# THE 5-HOUR AUTHOR™

Jeanette —

Here's to getting your game-changing health know-how out of your brain = into a book super fast...

# THE 5-HOUR AUTHOR™

How to Author a Client-Getting Book in Just 5 Hours...

## Travis John

Travis John Agency LLC
Created In Florida

Copyright @ 2015 by Travis John Agency LLC

All rights reserved. No part of this book may be used or reproduced in any manner whatsoever.

Disclaimer:
While a great deal of care has been taken to provide accurate and current information regarding the subject matter, the author, Travis John, and the company, Travis John Agency LLC, are not responsible for any errors or omissions or for the results obtained from the use of this information. The information contained in this book is intended to provide general advice and does not constitute legal, financial or other professional advice.

Information that was accurate as of the time of publication may become outdated by marketplace changes or conditions, new or revised laws, or other circumstances. Any slights against individuals, companies, or organizations are unintentional. All the examples in the book are based on assumptions no later in time than August 2015; thus, these assumptions are not guaranteed and may be subject to change. As with all assumptions and examples, results may vary based on a wide range of factors unique to each person's situation.

Some of the products and services mentioned in this book allow the author to receive compensation from the companies whose products are listed. You can rest easy knowing that anything the author recommends in this book is something he knows, likes and trusts. And that the fees for these resources have not been increased to compensate the author. In some cases, they have been reduced based on the author's relationship with these companies. As always, perform due diligence prior to any purchase you make.

Travis John Agency, LLC
Mail: 75 N. Woodward Avenue #81349
Tallahassee, FL 32313
Web: https://travisjohn.com
Email: travis@travisjohn.com
Schedule a Call: https://travisjohn.com/call

VERSION 1:

When you're done reading this book, I would like to get your feedback. Please send me an email to Travis+Author@TravisJohn.com and let me know what you think. Thanks!

# DEDICATION

*To all the business owners, entrepreneurs and independent professionals who can now author a client-getting book without all the fuss...*

# Contents

*Mission* xi

## Part I.
## The 5-Hour Author™

1. Author Of The Future 3
2. Your Decision 21
3. What's Holding You Back 31
4. My Journey 49
5. Add "Author" To Your Name 65
6. The 3 Ways To Get Clients 69
7. Getting Started 83
8. Step 1: Set Up Your Book 87
9. Step 2: Create Your Book 115
10. Step 3: Polish Your Book 129
11. Step 4: Publish Your Book 153
12. Step 5: Launch Your Book 161

## Part II.
## Bonus Section

13. Create An Audiobook   183
14. Authority To Author   191
15. Globalization   195
16. The Art Of Writing   197
17. It's Not Just For Books   201
18. Cross Promotion   203

*Return On Author (ROA)*   205
*5-Step Checklist*   208
*Tools and Resources*   216
*Acknowledgements*   223
*About the Author*   225

# MISSION

My mission with the 5-Hour Author is to help already successful[1] business owners, entrepreneurs and independent professionals author their first client-getting book.

---

[1]. www.AlreadySuccessful.com

PART I

# THE 5-HOUR AUTHOR™

# AUTHOR OF
# THE FUTURE

---

> "The Author of the Future™ will no longer be described as a writer, but as a creator." – **Travis John**

**Dear Author of the Future,**

Thank you for your interest in the 5-Hour Author™. It always makes me feel good when I can connect with other like-minded biz owners.

I wish I could tell you that the 5-Hour Author is as wild or magical as the name implies. Sorry to let you down, but you won't find any Hocus Pocus here. This is a REAL plan to author a REAL book with REAL merit. It will also require REAL work, just much, much less of it than you think.

Yes, the 5-Hour Author is innovative and it's freakin' awesome, but there are NO gotchas here. What I'm going to share with you in this book is a *clear path* for you to be an author.

You already realize that being an author would attract more of the right-fit clients. In fact, there's no shortage of people telling you the advantages of being an author. I am one of them. It's definitely hard to argue with this advice, but it's easier SAID than DONE.

**Can you think of something that would have**

a greater long-term impact on your biz than being an author?

- Something that's targeted only to the clients you want to attract?
- Something that provides instant credibility, even if they don't read it?
- Something that gets your ideal clients undivided attention and builds such a high degree of trust they feel like they've known you for years?
- Something that can start more client-getting conversations without being too salesy?

I can't... And here's one reason WHY:

Most people would agree the number one reason people don't do business with someone is the lack of TRUST. And that it takes several months, even years, to develop trust and rapport with ideal clients. But a book is the ONE thing that has the potential to fast-forward your trust factor! With just one communication, it's possible to make your ideal clients feel like they've known you for years...

BUT the process of authoring a book is no small task because:

- You're not interested in writing or learning how to write.
- You don't want to hire a ghostwriter who's going to churn out some boilerplate crap.
- You ONLY want a high-end, high-quality book that your ideal clients are going to find valuable.

The good news is:

- This book is NOT about me teaching you to write, or persuading you to be a writer. It's 100% focused on making you an AUTHOR.
- This is not a weird ghostwriting experience, but you will need a professional writer to polish the content that you create through the 5-Hour Author process.

- This process will produce a book that's the same quality as the clients you want to attract.

Plus, you can implement this in your business right away, even if you are overwhelmed.

Why? Because you already have the expertise and the clients, the 5-Hour Author will merely be a tool to help you do what you're already doing—but better.

The 5-Hour Author is focused on outlining and drawing out your unique knowledge (through your VOICE), then packaging it in the very best format—a BOOK!

In summary, I am going to help you come up with the very best idea, a compelling offer, a book title and a cover that will make your book irresistible to your ideal client.

You'll invest 5 hours to create the rough draft of your book, and then utilize the tools, services and resources I have outlined in this book to take it from there...

Would you like to shortcut the path to being an author? Ensure that you have ALL of the right elements in your book to attract the "right fit" clients? And eliminate ALL of the logistical nightmares that come with authoring your book? The 5-Hour Author will do all of that!

...Now you can effectively polish, publish and market your first client-getting book without all the fuss—the book that you can write without writing.

## The Future of Books

Until recently, the system for authoring a book was broken. That is unless you were a writer yourself, or you wanted to invest an enormous amount of time in developing top-notch writing skills.

...And even if you were convinced that you should write a book or intrigued about writing a book, you weren't 100% sure that you could write one that would meet your expectations. But just because you're not a writer doesn't mean you shouldn't be an author!

**If it's not your genius, it shouldn't be your job.**

It's probably ridiculous to think that a professional writer is an expert at what you do, just like it's probably ridiculous to think you are a professional writer.

But how many times have you heard "You should write a book"? Too many to count... It's awful advice, but it's laced with good intentions. See, people give this advice all the time because they know authoring a book is a game changer. They just don't know what it takes to pull it off...

...Look, don't take this the wrong way. I'm not saying you can't write a great book. In fact, I know you can... But why would you consider it if you could become an Author of the Future instead? And have the power to control how your book is written—but without having to actually write it? Well, that's exactly what I'm going to share with you.

**...It's not your fault that you haven't authored a client-getting book.**

The reality is that business leaders like you haven't had many attractive options to author a book. For good reasons, the idea was always squashed as soon as it entered your mind because you knew there was just too much red tape.

Until NOW being an author has been mostly reserved for indie writers and writers seeking big book deals. But another, not so talked about option is to get a professional writer to rewrite something you have already created...

...Business owners tend to have mixed views about working with writers, but that's usually because the relationship is misunderstood and misused. Regardless of how you feel about working with professional writers, this is the BEST option to create a book without mastering writing yourself...

...Did you know that most nonfiction books that are worth more than the paper they are printed on are either authored or co-authored by a professional writer? Many times you wouldn't even know this is the case because these writers elect not to receive public recognition for the writing they do.

Why is this? Because most people are not writers.

And frankly, already successful biz owners, entrepreneurs and independent professionals know that hiring a professional writer will be the ONLY way to publish the caliber of book on which they would be proud to have their name prominently displayed. They also know their ideal clients expect them to get some professional help writing a book. Simply put, they're comfortable being the expert, not the writer.

Not very long ago, niche books just didn't make good business sense.

The ONLY way you could get top-notch writing was to invest lots of time trying to find the perfect writer, and then invest large sums of money (plus royalties on future sales) to get a book written. But even with BIG stakes, many biz owners still jump at the opportunity to author a book that has "client getting" superpowers. That is, if they have an iron-clad idea and they can meticulously craft an outline and offer that will make their book a client-getting magnet. But even if they are willing to pay top dollar and know how to set up their book for SUCCESS, it still requires them to be belly to belly with their writer for several months. That is, if they want to ensure they have a quality book that's also going to goose their bottom line.

The reasons many of the top business leaders didn't write their own books are the same reasons you shouldn't. Just like you, they did not have the time or the writing skills to produce the kind of writing they wanted and deserved. For already successful business owners, professional writing services have been absolutely invaluable. But they had one "golden rule" when it came to authoring their book, which is the same rule you have. You want a writer who will write your book the way you want it written, but better than you could write it yourself.

The reality is, good writers will do a much better job, and do it significantly faster, than you would yourself—provided they have the proper DIRECTION.

**And that's where the problem lies with many writing experiences…**

…Just because a professional writer can write better than you doesn't mean he or she will write your book the way you want it written. Which is why most writing projects, particularly books, are doomed to fail before they start.

For a professional writer to write a book the

way you want it written, he or she will have to DEEPLY:

- Understand the vision for your book project.
- Understand your topic and content areas.
- Understand your natural tone and style, so he or she can speak in your voice.
- Understand the structure of your business, from soup to nuts.

Obviously, this would require you to spend an enormous amount of time with your writer. You would need to train this person to "temporarily" become an expert at what you do. But when you create your book's rough draft FIRST, using your voice. The writer does not have to spend time trying to master your voice. Or having to figure out the message you want to convey, because it's already right there, in your draft.

That's where the 5-Hour Author comes in. It allows you to invest just 5 hours to author the rough draft of your book, and let a professional writer take it from there... When you take control and ownership of the process by creating your content first, your writer will naturally be able to rewrite your draft in your voice, instead of making an awkward attempt to become your voice.

**The 5-Hour Author allocates talent where it belongs.**

Now you can meet a professional writer where he's most productive, and ensure success in less time and for less money.

Once you select a writer who has expertise in writing content related to yours, you simply give him or her the vision for your project and clear requirements along with a rough draft of your book. From there, your writer will be able to master your voice and get a deep understanding of your tone and style and the exact message you want to convey to your ideal client. He or she can mirror your voice, literally. The end result is a book that's 100% YOU.

When used effectively, top writers will use their writing prowess to turn your spoken words into masterful written words. They will rewrite, clean up, format, restructure, improve flow and even instinctively weave in new content where it's needed.

**High-profile writing on steroids.**

Finally, there's a way to author a book that attracts your ideal clients without all the fuss.

- What used to focus on being a writer now focuses on being an author.
- What used to have all kinds of rules, red tape and royalties that dictated your success now lets you control the book-creation process and author a long-term client-getting asset.

The 5-Hour Author allows professional writers to stay in their comfort zone and do their best work... Simply put, your writer can focus on WRITING about your best work, so you can focus on DOING your best work.

These insights can be summed up by this quote from money expert Loral Langemeier: "Strengthen your strengths and hire your weaknesses."

## Everything Is Possible

The 5-Hour Author would not be possible without the services that I have outlined in this book. As an Author of the Future™[1], you can now fast-track the authoring process because of better technology, more innovation and the rapid adoption of crowdsourced and productized services [2].

Instead of hiring the high-level talent you need full time. You can now share executive-level talent[3] and avoid the costly and time-consuming nature of hiring employees. The end result is that we no longer have to

---

[1]. www.AuthorOfTheFuture.com
[2]. www.ProductizedService.com
[3]. www.SharedExecutives.com

hunt—long and far—to find the best talent. In the sharing economy, much of the legwork has already been done for us...

...And, arguably, even better is how lightning fast you can engage crowdsourced talent. It used to take tons of time and red tape to sort out the scope of work, pricing, contract negotiations, etc. Now all you have to do is tell one platform your requirements and click the "buy now" button.

- What used to require an employee with a hefty salary now has a "buy now" button.
- What used to take weeks to find the best service providers now has a "buy now" button.
- What used to take long hours to negotiate now has a "buy now" button.
- What used to be labeled as "custom work" now has a "buy now" button.

Finally, you can get custom-made services with nearly the click of a button! There's no more back and forth with multiple vendors for weeks before you even get started. The transcriptionist, translator, proofreader, professional writer, book editor, graphic designer and book publisher (and dozens of other skilled workers and C-level executives) are all right here, at our fingertips.

Because change is continuous, I continually remind myself of the amazing world I am a part of (and should be contributing to daily).

- What used to be "the impossible" is now "possible whenever I like."
- What used to take months or years to accomplish can be accomplished in weeks, even hours.

Innovation is at every turn, and I'm truly appreciative to be a part of it...

...Now with crowdsourcing you can share all the best minds, talent and genius in the world, giving you no excuses not to author a book... Let's GO.

# YOUR DECISION

Congratulations On Your Decision To Be An Author.

Most business owners realize the benefits of becoming an author. In fact, they already have an idea for a book—a unique perspective, specialized knowledge, product or service they want to share. But it's their belief that they would have to spend hours and hours locked up in a room—WRITING.

That's just not true.

With the 5-Hour Author you can discover how to create, deploy and market your first "client getting" book in just 5 steps. It starts with investing just 5 hours of your time to author the rough draft of your book. And NO long hours writing, NO weird rules, NO publishing red tape and NO need for best-seller lists.

YES, really!

**It does sound outrageous, BUT it's outrageously Doable.**

So, how is it possible to author a book in just 5 hours? In this book, I am going to share with you *HOW* it is possible, and then I'm going to give you a complete step-by-step plan to author a *REAL* book for your business (including the exact tools and services that you can use to turn your book into a client-getting magnet).

Sound good? Good.

## Here's A Snapshot Of What We're Going To Cover:

Step 1 — How to draw out your very best idea, polish it and organize it into the best possible format.

Step 2 — How to get your book's content out of your brain and create the rough draft of your book. Hint: you'll do this by talking about your idea (just being yourself).

Step 3 — How to convert your spoken words into written words, and finding the perfect writer for you. How to work with a professional writer to re-write, add-to, tweak, polish, edit and elegantly marry all the parts together.

Step 4 — How to make the inside and outside of your book look professional and congruent with your message and your style (so your ideal client can't resist the opportunity to get a copy). Then how to finalize and publish your book as an ebook and paperback book.

Step 5 — How to get clients with your new book.

If you follow my plan, you will be able to shortcut the authoring process and produce a quality book for your business that will start (or continue) more conversations with your ideal clients. Period.

Simply put, the 5-Hour Author is the BEST way to author a client-getting book (super-fast) that will increase your businesses reach and revenue.

And a few more people may recognize you when you're in the grocery store.

## Who This Is For

The 5-Hour Author is designed for the majority of biz owners, entrepreneurs and independent professionals who don't like to write, don't have the time to write, don't know where to start or don't even have the time to figure out ALL the things necessary to author a successful client-getting book.

I used to believe the authoring process had to be difficult, time-intensive and extremely expensive… But after authoring my first business book (mostly the hard way), I discovered a much better (and more effective) way to be an author.

Everyone has a unique message to share, and my goal with the 5-Hour Author is to make that a reality!

It's about time for you to get your unique knowledge out of your brain and into a book. Start opening new doors and more conversations that grow your biz and get you more clients… ones you actually WANT.

**In fact, you already know the 5-Hour Author is RIGHT for you because…**

- You already realize the benefits of being an author.
- You already have a book inside you that's ready to get out.
- You have a unique perspective.
- You're successful at what you do.

- You're ready to invest 5 hours to author the draft of your book.

On the other hand, this is not for you if...

- You're not accepting new clients.
- You prefer to get clients the same way you always have.
- You don't want to get paid more because you're an author.

The 5-Hour Author really works the best if you...

1) **You have a real business.** The 5-Hour Author is for biz owners and business owners, entrepreneurs and independent professionals who know their STUFF. Simply put, you're an expert at what you do.

2) **Your business is a high-value professional service "relationship type" business.** You have a high profit margin per client or you sell high-priced, big-ticket items or have a high lifetime customer value. The 5-Hour Author doesn't work well for businesses that

sell on a highly transactional basis (as opposed to transformational and relational) or that sell a low-priced commodity item.

For example, this works great for most professional services and several industries like real estate, financial services, law, insurance, accounting, manufacturing, engineering, distribution, high-priced and high-end products, consulting, coaching, speaking, high tech and software businesses. This works for almost all medical and health care businesses like chiropractic, dental and podiatry. It also works well for niche product and service providers like business growth consultants, education leaders, career and employment agencies and advisors, self-help gurus, health and fitness experts, beauty advice and many, many more industry leaders...

3) **You don't care if you don't make any money from selling copies of your book.** The real income and value from authoring a book will come from the clients you get, usually called the backend sales. A good rule of

thumb is it should take only one client, patient or deal to make this worth your time and investment.

4) **You are ready to invest in your business.** When you follow the 5-Hour Author plan, the total cost to complete your book will be around $3,000. This will vary, but largely depends on what you pay a professional writer to rewrite your book's draft. The stakes to be an author are high, but so are the rewards. This small investment now will pay you dividends for many years to come

5) **You are committed.** If you want the title of AUTHOR attached to your name, you'll have to be committed to completing your book. You can do this as fast as you want to and get as much help as you need... The only constant is that you will invest 5 hours to author the rough draft of your book.

When you follow the process, you'll be able to author a high-quality book in about 8 weeks, even if you already have a hectic schedule. As the saying goes, "Rome wasn't built in a day," and building a client-getting book is no different. The key to success is once you start the process, don't stop.

Will this work for you? I hope so.

Up next, we'll figure out what's really holding you back from being an author (I bet they're the same things that held me back).

When we're done with the next chapter, you'll understand WHY you can't wait another day to be an author...

# WHAT'S HOLDING YOU BACK

"Whenever you find your self on the side of the majority, it is time to pause and reflect." – Mark Twain

## There Are 4 Main Reasons Most Professionals Will NEVER Author A Book:

1) They don't know where to START...

2) They don't know HOW to do it...

3) They don't have TIME to do it...

4) They don't want to be a WRITER...

Well, it may seem too good to be true, but the 5-Hour Author solves all 4 of these problems.

The 5-Hour Author—surprise!—takes only 5 hours of your time to author your book's draft. And you don't have to know HOW to do anything, because I have provided a step-by-step plan (just for you) in this book.

I even took it ONE step further.

In addition to the 4 reasons why most people don't become an author, I have identified the 11 "logical lies" (false beliefs about becoming an author) that kill everyone else's dreams of authoring a book...

I know these logical lies are the problem because I used to believe all the same things. But after authoring my first book (mostly the hard way), I discovered a much better (and more effective) way to be an author.

When I'm done explaining, you'll understand WHY you can't wait another day to be an author. Seriously.

## Here Are The 11 Logical Lies:

1) **Size matters.** In the case of books, most people believe bigger is better. But the truth is your ideal client doesn't care how long your book is. He just wants the benefit you're promising on the cover and the information that's between the covers...

But there's just one caveat where size does matter, and it's for FIRST impressions, particularly when you're sharing a paperback book. So it is my belief that your book needs to meet your ideal clients' usual and customary expectations of what constitutes a real BOOK.

That's where the 5-Hour Author comes in. I designed this process to help you draw out your best message and package it as a book that uniquely represents you and the clients YOU want to attract. A book (and size) that you're proud to share with your most discerning clients, but doesn't take years off your life to create.

The 5-Hour Author process will produce a paperback book that's the perfect length for paperback and digital books, a book that delivers just the right balance of education and substance without any fluff. Even more important, it's the perfect size to effectively share ONE thing with your ideal clients that you want them to either understand or believe (from your unique knowledge) about a problem they have, a solution you provide or an opportunity they wouldn't want to miss out on... By sharing your message in an easy-to-digest format, you can provide just enough information (which your ideal client can read in 1 hour) to have that client ready to start, restart or continue a conversation with you.

By contrast, when a book is too short it provides a shallow reading experience resulting in poorly defined topics, theory-based content or a sales message disguised as a book. The book I'm talking about is a perfect example of a high-end, high-value book that's laser focused on sharing ONE thing with the exact clients that you want to attract.

2) **I have to be a writer.** Everyone seems to believe that being an author requires writing. Not always. The goal here is to spend time being an AUTHOR, not a WRITER. It is my belief that you should write like you speak and this starts with getting your message out through your VOICE. The best way to create the rough draft of your book is to simply record yourself talking about your best stuff, and then transcribe it into text. This is done

after you've decided on your best idea and created the outline and the questions that your book will answer. Of course, once you've created your rough draft a professional writer will polish and organize your message into the best possible format.

Even If you enjoy writing, the 5-Hour Author is simply a head start to create your book's rough draft.

3) **Books have to be written a certain way.** How you create your book's content and format doesn't matter. It just has to flow and have value to the reader. The 5-Hour Author is simply a blueprint to draw out your best stuff through your voice – as if you're sitting down talking with your ideal client in person. The result is a book that's 100% unique to you. One that lets your personality and style SHINE. Embrace this format. Your clients will love it.

4) **Publishing red tape.** Self-publishing is here for good. And with the many advanced self-publishing tools and services available today,

the inside and outside of your book will look better than those of most best sellers. In fact, some best sellers use these same tools and platforms. The end result is a kick-ass book that is ready for EVERY bookstore (online and offline).

5) **Hit a "best seller" list.** Every time I turn around there's another guru touting ways to become a "best seller." The truth is, it doesn't flipping matter for 99% of business owners – you just want clients! Sure, a best seller can skyrocket your clients, too, but that process is usually time- and money-intensive and a complete crapshoot. The truth is simple: MOST of your clients will come from the effective use of direct marketing. This begins with integration of your book (strategically) into all your biz touch points – not from spending several months and thousands of dollars trying to get your book on some best-seller list. Hey, the reality is your book will be best-seller caliber. So if it happens, great. But focus your time, energy and resources on

being a best client-getting author not a best-selling author.

6) **I need testimonials on the back cover.** Don't waste time on testimonials. So many people get hung up on this. I have to restrain lots of anger when I think about the whole testimonials, reviews, social-proof game. Don't get me wrong; it is important to have social proof. But it's just become so fake. It's annoying. So, here's my 2 cents on testimonials...

You don't need them if you can PROVE, in advance, to your ideal client that you can help him. You do this by delivering such an outstanding amount of value in your book that there's no doubt you're the person that the client wants to do business with.

Third-party proof is usually better than testimonials. (Use a trusted third-party news source and cite that story or angle in support of your service, product, point of view, etc.)

There are even federal laws that regulate the

use of testimonials. Depending on what kind of biz you're in, it could be a bit like walking on egg shells.

The bottom line is your ideal client will want a copy of your book because of one reason: They want to get the benefit you are offering on the front cover (not because of the testimonials on the back cover).

If you have testimonials, great, use them. But don't put them on the back cover. The back cover of your book should be reserved 100% for how you're going to help the reader.

7) **Do I really have something unique to share?** Sure you do. Everybody has something unique to share. One of my favorite quotes is from Gary Bencivenga, the legendary copywriter. "Stand for something and you will never stand alone." It says it all. Your ideal clients want to hear what YOU have to say, what you specialize in and what you know. And your book should be 100% focused around using your unique knowledge to educate your ideal client. That's it.

... Actually, once you give it a little thought, you'll probably realize there are multiple things that you have a unique perspective on...

8) **Making money from my book.** Don't worry about how much you're going to make in book sales because the real income and value of being an author don't come from selling copies of your book. Nope, it will come from the clients you get, usually called the backend sales.

The job of your client-getting book is to start or continue the conversation with your ideal client. Your book will lead the conversation to your product or service. Plus, it should take only one deal (maybe two) to make the 5-Hour Author worth your time. That's why one of the best ways to use your book is to just give it away for free in exchange for your ideal clients contact information.

Either way, my philosophy on front-end book sales is to invest any money you make in marketing. If you can make enough book sales to break-even on what it costs to acquire a new client then you're WAY ahead of the game...

9) **People won't read my book.** That's right, (most) people won't read your book. But that's okay. WHAT? Just because most of the people won't *actually* read your book doesn't mean they won't want to do business with you. Many of your ideal clients will want to talk to you strictly because they want the BENEFIT you are promising ON THE COVER of your book. That's it.

Plus, you should be authoring your book for the 5% who really matter anyway. TALK to the 5% who care. They will be your raving fans. And when they read your book, the choice to do business with you will be obvious.

10) **A book won't work for ME.** Hogwash. If you have a real business (and you actually talk to your clients), then a book is for you. Use your client-getting book to educate someone on your unique process, system,

service or product. You may want to show someone how to solve a specific problem, or you might highlight a solution that you can provide. Or you can share the process clients will go through when they choose to work with you.

Your ideal client wants to be educated about what YOU know. It may even seem boring or uninteresting to you; but that's because you do it every day. Your ideal client will gobble up your book when he's in the market for what you do or sell. It's that simple.

Plus, you'll be attracting the people you want to do business with and repelling the ones who are not a fit. This alone will skyrocket productivity because the book will do some of the hard work for you.

Thus, being a 5-Hour Author will lead to more QUALITY conversations (and more quality conversations = more money).

Here are a few qualifying questions to ask yourself:

- Do your ideal clients read books?
- Do your clients ask questions that are related to problems they have or solutions you provide? Are these topics you could share in a book?
- Do your clients brag about the results and transformations they've experienced from working with you?
- Are there unique attributes about your product, service, biz or methodology that, if shared, would be extremely valuable to your ideal clients?
- Are there interesting things you could share that would clearly differentiate you from your competition?
- Do you offer unique experiences, such that your ideal clients would jump at the opportunity to get

involved if they actually knew about them?

11) **I've got to do tons of research, use big data and impress people with my credentials.** Obviously, the 5-Hour Author is not for research-intensive books, which take WAY more than 5 hours to author. My advice is if you can't quote something off the top of your head, then it's probably not something you need to include in a client-getting book. The whole point of the 5-Hour Author is to package an intimate conversation with your ideal client avatar and then use it to reach MORE ideal clients.

You just want to draw out your unique knowledge through your voice, and when you do this effectively, you'll capture yourself at "concert pitch," getting all your best stuff out of your brain and into your book.

Even if your business relies heavily on data, this DATA is NOT the reason why prospects initially raise their hand to get your help. Nope, these facts, figures and big data are not the *real* reason they're attracted to you (or your business) in the first place. The truth is your ideal clients don't care about the DATA until they know you care about them AND that you can actually help them. Sure, this information is superimportant, so here's my advice. Once you're done creating the rough draft for your book, if you think plugging in a few stats, third-party proof or resources will enhance your book, then go ahead and work with your writer to weave them into your book. But I believe that most of your data points will be more impactful (and more appropriate) during your first phone call or meeting, after you have warmed them up with your book.

## The Bottom Line

The 5-Hour Author helps you draw out your BEST thinking so you can share ONE thing that you already know, something that delivers awesome value and that naturally leads into your service or product.

It's the perfect setup for you to get more business because its easy-to-digest (and prestigious) format pulls your ideal clients toward you (like a huge magnet) by simply offering to help them at the end of the book...

NOW, Is the Time

Now you can share your unique knowledge, specialized experience, product or service with your ideal clients through a book. You can do this by investing just 5 hours of your time.

*Don't let logical lies hold you back from being an author.*

- Or discount the effectiveness of a client-getting book...
- Or discount the impact a client-getting book will have on your biz.
- Or let the simplicity of the 5-Hour Author scare you off...

I think by now it's clear to you that every biz owner needs a book working for his or her biz. It's truly the cheapest salesperson you could ever HIRE!

So, if you're accepting new clients, you shouldn't wait another day to add a book to your biz.

Because a book is simply a vehicle for you to achieve bigger goals and have a bigger future...

If that's what YOU want, I'm going to show you how, *exactly*, to get new clients with your book.

**I have put together a 5-step plan just for you. Keep reading and then let me know what you think.**

But before we get into the plan, I'm going to share with you a few more things that will help you understand why the 5-Hour Author happened, AND some of the key benefits of being a 5-Hour Author.

# MY JOURNEY

## Why The 5-Hour Author Happened

I've always been interested in how things are made or how they came to be. So I'm sharing this story with you. Unfortunately for me, I played the leading role in this one.

In one way, the creation of the 5-Hour Author is a typical story of how I had a problem and just spent some time figuring it out... and then fixed it.

On the other hand, it's a little crazy how this all went down. So I have decided to share it with you.

**Here goes.**

It all started when I was doing my first book, mostly alone, and mostly the hard way…

You see, authoring a book didn't come easy to me, and I spent more time than I probably should have figuring this stuff out. So I spent a lot of time, yep, you guessed it, sitting in front of my computer.

That's not unusual, right? Well, at age 40, I guess my body didn't appreciate the long hours of inactivity. I've always been a healthy dude…

NOT anymore!

So, what happened next was I got sick, not from stress, but physically sick from (what I believe was) sitting at the computer, you guessed it, for hours and hours and hours at a time…

And not taking breaks like you're supposed to.

Without getting into too much detail, I literally developed all kinds of weird issues internally, and after a few months of tests (of all kinds)... *supposedly* nothing was wrong with me.

**But I was not okay.**

Fortunately for me (and admittedly out of desperation), I was able to connect with a natural-healing doctor who pretty quickly identified a low-grade infection in my gut. (This is the simple way of explaining it; I won't get into the details here.)

So after a few months of juicing and eating only good, raw food (along with regular trips to my chiropractor and a few natural remedies), I began to heal my gut, and finally started to get better. Whew.

Anyway, I really believe all that sitting messed me up. So what did I do then?

## It Was Time For A Breakthrough

The old me and the new me had a long talk, and we figured out that this sitting in front of a screen all day every day would not work out so well in the long run.

So I let my entrepreneurial spirit run wild, and began reverse-engineering the author process (that I'd already spent too long trying to figure out). I now focused on finding ways to shortcut the process and all the crap that comes with trying to publish a book. I just wanted to come up with a simple process that I could use to author a great book much, much faster.

I did this because I knew a book was the best platform to share my message, get a little more credibility along the way, get some celebrity status (if I were lucky) and maybe one-up a few competitors.

So I wasn't going to throw in the towel. But

how do you author a book and not write for long hours?

You can now!

After much tweaking and lots of thinking sessions and trials, the 5-Hour Author was born as a quick (and effective) way to become an author and share your unique knowledge... with people you can actually help.

So I started off by deconstructing the process used by the most successful writers, because I didn't want to reinvent the wheel—I just wanted to make the wheel move much, much faster... And ultimately what I figured out was how to harness the magic of writing just like you speak without all the time commitment. Here's how it went down...

First, What I Was Doing Right

One of the first things I discovered when I got into writing was how to write the way I speak. This method of writing resonated with me because I felt it was the best way to harness my unique voice and, frankly, it was the most natural to me. In studying writing, specifically direct response copywriting, I discovered quickly that this type of writing style was for ME. One of the writers I am fascinated by is the great Gary Halbert. I really love his edgy style and his overall approach to writing. The biggest takeaway I got from him and other writers was so simple it could easily be discounted. It was just be yourself and write like you speak. For me the end result was writing that is authentic, usually conversational and even informal at times. But it was me, and it worked.

I really believe that writing like you speak is the only way to write. When you make the decision to write like you speak, it's much easier to find your unique voice (and style) and, more important, you'll capture all your best stuff and effectively communicate your message. The stuff that people actually want to read about!

Although this writing method was working for me, I needed to figure out how to write faster.

## Here's What I Uncovered

Of course, I knew that writing was time-intensive and required lots (and lots) of editing. But what I found out was interesting. Even people who LIKE to write struggle with the writing process because they try to EDIT while they are writing. I also found out that the best writers go to great lengths to keep themselves from editing while they write. See, the best writers in the world already know that editing while writing is a huge NO-NO that leads to many unproductive sessions and adds more hours to the writing process. But WHY it's a no-no is not because of the unproductivity it brings, though that is a good reason; it's because when you try to do both at the same time, you're interrupting the flow that's important to the creative writing process. The deep thinking and focus that you achieve when you don't edit while you write are the SECRETS to tapping into your expertise and sucking your unique knowledge out of your brain. When it's done effectively, all your best thoughts and ideas will come to the surface.

No surprise, I was constantly editing while I was writing and interrupting my flow and killing my creative thinking, thus not getting my best stuff out of my brain. And it gets worse; after analyzing my writing I found out that I was spending much more time editing than I was actually writing. I did find out this is normal, which made me feel a little better, but it was depressing nonetheless.

So I dug a little deeper into how to effectively write without editing. The basic concept is to throw ALL the rules of writing out the window and just write freely. That means you don't worry about grammar, sentence structure, capitalization, punctuation—anything. You don't do any editing at all; you just write. And when we let go of these rules, the results are truly liberating.

After adopting this new technique with my writing, I was instantly more creative and productive.

For example, my favorite writing tip to keep me in the flow state came from Neil Strauss. It's a simple thing he calls "To Come" or TK. Anytime you don't know what you're going to say, or you're stuck on anything at all. You don't stop what you're doing or take the time to research or even think about it. Just type "TK," which means to come—this is the stuff you'll fill in at a later time. The reason it's TK and not TC is because there are no words or spell-checking associated with TK. So you can easily go back to all your TKs in any word processing application and finish your work at a later time.

But this edit-free experimentation was more than a new way of writing (and thinking). It led me to a much bigger breakthrough.

Actually, it hit me like a ton of bricks. "What if I just decided to write like I speak but do it literally, actually just speak what I want to write then edit what I said?"

## Here Comes The Breakthrough

Since I was already writing like I speak and not editing while I write, what if I just went ahead and skipped the writing and went right to speaking?

Well, that's exactly what I did.

I realized that the natural thing to do was to draw out my best thinking through my voice by just talking. I love to talk (ask anyone who knows me), and truth be told, I have always been a better verbal communicator anyway.

So after some necessary testing and tweaking, I found I could draw out what I wanted to write (my best stuff) through my voice. This was really a natural next step for me because I already was writing like I spoke; now I just added rocket fuel. Plus I felt like the shackles that attached me to my desk for long hours were suddenly removed. On top of that, this new way of thinking and doing was a pathway to more freedom and productivity because I was able to get content out of my brain at lightning speed. But I was also able to avoid the huge editing trap that I constantly fell into.

What I did was take the best practices of writing, married them and simply added a much-needed time shortcut. Instead of writing the way I speak, I chose to speak the way I wanted to write, so I could be 100% sure to draw out my best thinking but in less time. By choosing to write like I speak (literally) and just record everything I say, I could harness ALL my creative gems in one shot. One way to do this is use Rev Voice Recorder (more on this in Chapter 9) and then submit the file to be transcribed into writing.

That's (in my opinion) why this process works so well. It's the intersection of all the best ways to get your unique knowledge and perspective out of your brain and into a book the first time around. You really need to just speak and record everything you say, and then transcribe it into writing.

When done effectively, there is less editing because you just let it flow…

Of course, the process of recording what you want to write is not a new concept. In fact, people have been doing it for years (including me), but I never went deep enough with the process or applied it to the creation of a book. One catalyst that helped me get clear on the power of recording your voice was hearing Dean Jackson of I Love Marketing talk about his book-creation process.

**Sharing what I learned with others.**

I applied this same type of "breakthrough thinking" to my entire book-creation process. Of course, this process wasn't called the 5-Hour Author originally. It was just the process I used to write my own books faster. But after putting this process to the test, I realized that it was entirely too valuable to keep to myself. After I made a few more tweaks, I had a process that I was proud to tell others about. And there's no better way to get the word out than through a BOOK...

Once I decided to share this process with others, I had to come up with a name that was fitting and had the marketing muscles to make everyone want to get a copy. The 5-Hour Author name is perfect because it clearly explains the main benefit you'll get, it's descriptive and it ignites curiosity.

## But There Is A Catch

Of course, the key to making this work is the SET UP. As you know, all forms of writing have a period of brainstorming and planning, and the 5-Hour Author is no different. Nothing weird, but there is ONE major caveat: You MUST be prepared before you begin free-flow speaking. This doesn't involve scripting out what you're going to say—not at all. What I mean is you've got to set up the outline of what you want to say and in what order. By doing this you'll be able to quickly and painlessly create the right flow for your book and speak freely. This process allows you to break up what you're going to talk about into bite-size chunks so you can easily follow a logical path.

The other catch is obvious, but I'll point this out just in case there are any knuckleheads who get a copy of this book. This process won't work unless you actually know WHAT you're talking about. That means you've got to be an expert at the topic you want to discuss.

That's it.

Stay tuned, because I'm going to show you how to follow the setup process (in great detail) in Chapter 8, Step 1, of the 5-Hour Author.

## One More Thing

I still like to write, but sitting for long hours is unhealthy. So I had to find a way to work without sitting as much. Naturally, one way I have done this is by taking more breaks. The other way that works for me is using a standing desk. You can see my standing desk at 5HourAuthor.com/Standing-Desk. C'est la vie.

Now let's get into some of the key benefits of being an author. Come along...

# ADD "AUTHOR" TO YOUR NAME

In the next couple of chapters I'll share with you the most valuable tips and benefits of authoring your first book. A book that pulls your ideal clients toward you like a huge invisible force field.

I thought it would be good to kick off this Chapter with a few tidbits that will give you some perspective on the benefits and elite status that come along with being an author.

I'm doing this because it's always best to see the big picture before deciding to dive into anything. That's exactly what this chapter is about.

Sure, most people already agree that a book is one of the best platforms to share a message.

But why is this, really?

Because a book positions you as The EXPERT.

And one of the biggest benefits of being an author is the instant credibility it brings and, sometimes, the celebrity effect it has.

The end result is it will *open new doors for you* that would have taken years to open otherwise. Or would never have been opened at all.

It sounds weird to say it this way, but a book gives you "client getting" superpowers because it shows *goodwill and instantly builds rapport* with your prospective clients.

These superpowers allow you to help more people because you'll be attracting clients who actually want (and need) the services and products you offer.

And being an author gives you the opportunity to charge a premium for your expertise.

Plus, it's timeless; a book is an asset that will get you clients for years to come...

Now with the 5-Hour Author, you can create and deploy a client-getting book in your biz quickly and painlessly... making it easy to add the title "Author" to your name.

And, secure an unfair advantage over your competition.

Now, let's talk money. In the next chapter I'll share with you the 3 ways to get clients with your book...

# THE 3 WAYS TO GET CLIENTS

In this chapter I'm going to give you the inside scoop on HOW, exactly, you can use your book to get (more) clients and grow profits.

After all, that is the reason you really want to author a book, right?

You don't want to be an author just because it's cool (although I know it's tempting)…

Before I get into the 3 ways to grow your profits, let me first restate why using a client-getting book is magical.

When used effectively, a book will give you more reach and more revenue (you'll reach more people and you'll make more money). That's it!

The primary job of your book is to start the conversation with your ideal client. Your book will then lead this conversation to your service or product.

BUT there are 3 ways to use your book to grow your profits and add new clients in a jiffy.

And because you're going to use it to educate your ideal client, you'll be attracting the people you want to do business with and repelling the ones who are not a fit. This alone will skyrocket productivity, because the book will do some of the hard work for you.

Thus, being a 5-Hour Author will lead to more QUALITY conversations. (More quality conversations = more money, in less time with less hassle.)

So, let's get started...

## Here Are The 3 Ways To Use Your Client-Getting Book To Goose Profits:

1) Use it to start a conversation.
2) Use it to further a conversation.
3) Use it to restart a conversation.

Sounds pretty straightforward, right?

*Now I'm going to demonstrate the 3 ways for you.*

**1) Use your book to start a conversation: Cold Leads**

This is the most common way to use a book. It's a way for you to position yourself as the celebrity, authority and specialist in your niche. To start the conversation with your ideal client you just have to get the book into your prospect's hands. You can easily have your prospects download it, you can email it or you can send them a physical copy.

The most popular way to generate new leads is to give away your ebook for free (or just charge the shipping costs for the paperback book). Of course, you'll do this in exchange for the prospect's name, email and possibly mailing address.

Of course, you'll need to use Marketing Muscles[1] to introduce the book to your ideal prospects. That means you'll need to craft a few successful ads to make it irresistible for them to grab a copy.

But only a small percentage of people that get your book will buy from you as a result of their first conversation. So it's important to have a system in place that allows you to

---

1. www.MarketingMuscles.com

channel the conversation toward a future sale. The key to exponential sales is your Conversation Channels[2]—what you say, how you say it, and when you say it, and which medium you use to say it. And fine tuning these conversation channels based on what each client wants. A simple formula to follow is to provide a tremendous amount of value FIRST (for free or for a small fee). Then invite your ideal clients to work with you. This approach makes it easy for your ideal clients to raise their hands when they're ready for your help.

When you take the time to build a Client-Getting Machine[3] around your book. You'll have a complete system that ebbs and flows with the engagement your clients and prospects have with you. Enabling you to invest more time with the people that want your help. And allowing you to attract ideal clients, build rapport and convert more high-value sales.

2. www.ConversationChannels.com
3. www.ClientGettingMachine.com

Let's get into how you can use your book to generate new leads.

There are many ways, but I'm only going to share a few of the most effective with you now...

...The first and very best way is to use a single-purpose webpage (landing page).

For example, at the time I'm writing this book the 5-Hour Author landing page, located at 5HourAuthor.com/Simple converts an average of 51% of all it's visitors to real prospects.

The way I've been able to achieve such a high conversion rate, compared to a 20% conversion rate, which most people would be happy with, is through lots of testing, tweaking and application of the methods I've learned from Dean Jackson, the creator of the first landing page.

Designing a successful landing page is a balance of art, neuroscience, timing and touch that starts by having something valuable to offer your ideal client. In this case, it's about having an irresistible book cover and title. The next key to success is to write the content on the landing page. This is WHAT you say and HOW you say it. And because the goal of this type of landing page is to keep it SIMPLE, what you DON'T say on the page is just as important to achieving higher conversions. The final key to success is mastering the "look and feel" of the landing page. Just as with the other components of this landing page, when it comes to your design, less is more.

A great way to piggyback on your books webpage is to create a direct mail letter and/or postcard that is sent to a highly targeted list of ideal clients. The mailing piece would direct the prospect to your webpage to get a free copy of your book.

If you already have a mailing list, awesome. If you're looking for more options, check out http://lists.nextmark.com.

The next thing that works very well is to create press opportunities, or "PR," that will open the doors for you to be featured as the expert.

I recommend that you reach out to other digital content publishers (website owners, blogs, podcasts and publications). You should also contact more traditional media like TV, print and radio.

You can also use press release distribution services; for example, here are three easy to use and highly effective web-based PR services:

- PR Web www.prweb.com
- iReach by PR Newswire ireach.prnewswire.com
- WebWire www.webwire.com

Once you get PR, the real benefits will come from MARKETING the PR you just got.

I call this Remarketing PR[4]. It's taking your

---

[4]. www.RemarketingPR.com

high-credibility, newsworthy PR and then remarketing it to your customers and prospects by email, on your website, via pay-per-click ads, banner ads, social networks, etc. This is truly where the PR gold is realized.

A sweet tool for remarketing your PR and converting more sales is Sniply.▬. It allows you to embed a call-to-action on every link and page you share.

You'll also want to give out your book at trade shows, events, mastermind meetings, speaking engagements and presentations.

Then there are the online retailers like Amazon, Apple, Barnes & Noble, etc. Selling in these places is an excellent way to get A LOT of exposure for your book (and your biz). This option is particularly great if you service clients from all over.

If you're a local business, you may or may not get the same benefits by using these mass-marketing platforms. As always, it's best to look at how this will fit into your business goals and your marketing plan before pursuing this option.

Up next...

## 2) Use your book to further a conversation: Warm leads

As you know, it's just as hard to keep a conversation going (especially when you're trying to keep it moving toward a sale) as it is to get new prospects. The real money is on NO because most prospects will not be ready to work with you right away. That's why a book plays a critical role in getting (and keeping) the attention on why you're the best and only option your prospect should consider when the time is right for them.

Plus, it will help you sell without being too salesy.

Because your book is an educational asset, it will work wonders for you as a presales tool (to educate your prospect prior to a call or in-person meeting). This helps warm up your prospect and position you as the expert.

Another method is to use the book as a leave-behind or takeaway (AFTER you have had your first phone call, online meeting or in-person meeting with the prospect).

One more way is to identify joint venture partners, vendors and other raving fans that would mutually benefit by helping you get more exposure for your book. When you structure it as a win-win and find the right partners, this method can have the greatest impact on your bottom line.

Onward...

**3) Use your book to restart a conversation: Hot leads**

We've all been guilty of neglecting our current clients, past clients and the so-called dead leads. Your book is the quickest and easiest way to get back in touch and restart meaningful conversations.

Here's why:

It's likely that your book will educate them on something new or something different (than what they have shown interest in or bought in the past).

Or your product or service has improved in some way.

Or you've added new products and services.

Either way, a book is an excellent reason to reconnect with your current clients, past clients and prospects, and to revive dead leads. You'll get more conversations restarted, which will lead to them buying more from you and spending more money with you, and making more frequent purchases.

All you have to do is notify your current list by phone, text message, email, or direct mail, then follow the same nurture process you use for new leads.

This chapter was intended to get you thinking about the many ways you can start, continue or revive conversations.

I'm sure you are thinking of more ways to use your book right now. Get creative, and embed your book into all your biz touch points.

How else can you use your client-getting book to help you sell without selling?

Now it's time for us to get to work on your new book. In the next Chapter I'll introduce you to the 5-step plan you'll need to follow to author your first book, then we'll jump right into it...

Let's get started... Cool? Cool.

# GETTING STARTED

## 5 Hours. 5 Steps. Unlimited New Clients.

Now you can share your unique knowledge, specialized experience, product or service with your ideal clients through a book. You can do this by investing just 5 hours of your time to author the rough draft of your book.

When you follow my advice (and trust the

5-Hour Author plan), you will be able to shortcut the authoring process and produce a quality book for your business that will start, continue or re-start more conversations with your ideal clients. Period.

As you've probably heard before, 80% of SUCCESS comes from the setup or preparation stage of your project. Being an author is—surprise—no different.

Eighty percent of the success you will have with this project will be from the work you do in Step 1, the setup phase.

So, without further ado, let's dive in.

**Here's a breakdown of your 5-step plan:**

Step 1: The perfect setup process, and identifying your superpowers.

Step 2: The process of getting the information out of your brain and into a book.

Step 3: The process of converting your spoken words to written words, and finding the perfect writer for you. The rewriting process, and polishing your work of art.

Step 4: The final steps, cover design and publishing your shiny new book.

Step 5: The launch of your book into the world by getting the word out.

# STEP 1: SET UP YOUR BOOK

> "Good writing is clear thinking made visible." – **Bill Wheeler**

# The perfect setup process, and identifying your superpowers.

# Time Invested — 3 Hours

**Action steps:**

1) The purpose of your book.

2) The very best idea for your book (what's your book going to be about?).

3) The questions your book will answer (what's the ONE thing you want your ideal client to believe or understand?).

4) The ideal client avatar (with WHOM (exactly) you want to have a conversation in your book).

5) The outline, topics and format that will provide an optimum reader experience.

6) Niche down (polish and organize your topics into the best possible format).

7) The interview questions that you will answer in Step 2.

8) Draw out the most compelling offer for your book (how you or your product can help your ideal client).

9) The perfect title for your book.

You'll spend an hour coming up with a draft that includes these action items and the second hour polishing them and the final hour finalizing them. For maximum benefits use the entire 3 hours.

Okay, let's go...

## What's The Purpose Of Your Book?

I know there are a couple of things getting in the way of your starting your book.

... It's deciding on WHAT you're really going to do with your book and WHAT it's actually going to be about.

You're 100% right. Defining the purpose of your book AND the idea for your book are super important, and I completely understand why they could be getting in your way...

That's why I put this exercise together: for you to spend some time thinking, specifically, what your purpose and your goals are for this project, AND the very best idea for your book—before you get started.

When you're done you'll have more clarity and confidence to move forward with your book.

But I'm sure this will get your creative juices flowing.

**Finding your purpose**

The only way to author a "good" book (or create any project for that matter) is to embrace the almost clichéd saying: "Start with the end in mind."

By "getting clear" on the purpose of your

book and why you are doing this, you will have immediate clarity that will get you pumped to do your book project.

Ask yourself: "What is the result I want to achieve?" (be very, very specific)

For example: Get 10 new clients in the next 6 months for X.

Once you know your purpose for authoring a book and what the desired outcome looks like for you, then it's time to come up with the IDEA for your book.

## The Perfect Idea

Now for the fun part. You need to decide WHAT your book is going to be about—the IDEA for your book.

Trying to determine your very best idea may seem overwhelming at first because more than one idea may come to mind.

- How do you pick the BEST one?

- What's the best one for you to pursue?
- Which one will have the greatest impact on your ideal client?
- Which one will have the greatest impact on your biz?

Here's the quickest and easiest way for you to get clear on WHAT your book should be about.

Make a list of your top 3 services or products (which is usually the ones that make you the most money). As you can imagine, a client-getting book will be most successful when you don't reinvent the wheel or try to create some brand-new market for yourself...

Okay. Now sort these services or products based on these 5 criteria.

1) What is the most unique and/or unique to you?

2) What is the easiest to fulfill?

3) What do you love to do/what are you most passionate about?

4) What can make you the most money?

5) What will have the greatest impact on your ideal client?

It shouldn't take long for you to see a clear winner. The winner will be what your book is about.

**What you're going to talk about in your book (the Outline and the Questions your book will answer)**

Now it is time to take that IDEA (you just got clear on) and go deeper with your THINKING.

You know WHAT (in general terms) book is going to be about, but now you've got to figure out the WHY.

**Ask yourself these questions:**

- Why is this topic the clear winner?

- Why is it unique?
- Why is this topic the easiest for me to talk about?
- Why am I passionate about this topic?
- Why is my related service or product the easiest for me to fulfill?
- Why do I make the most money from it?
- Why does this have the greatest impact on my ideal client?

Answering these questions about your IDEA will give you profound insight.

**Next, take a few minutes to get clear on WHO (exactly) you want to have a conversation with in your book.**

Of course, this is your prospect, the ideal client avatar that you want to reach with your book. The best way to do this is to define the exact avatar YOU want to speak to. You probably have a current or past client who is the exact person you'll want to imagine.

A good exercise is to make a list of ALL of their attributes—problems, goals, values, opportunities, age, income, education, demographics, gender, marital status, etc. Then make a list of the results and transformations they got (directly and indirectly) from working with you, or using your product or service.

If you're having trouble, a great way to get clear on your ideal client avatar is to envision yourself sitting down and talking with them one-on-one.

Once you've thoroughly documented your ideal client avatar ask yourself these questions:

- What is the most logical question my ideal client is going to be asking themselves (about this service or product I provide)?
- What can I say or share with this ideal client that would make them want to start a conversation with me?

Then I recommend using a technique I learned up from visionary and business growth expert, Mike Koenigs. Make a list of the 10 FAQs (frequently asked questions) your ideal clients have about your product, service or solution and the 10 should-ask questions (questions that they should ask you BUT they don't)...

## The Outline And Questions Your Book Will Answer

Congratulations! You have just created a rough draft of the OUTLINE and the QUESTIONS that your book will answer, the ones that will draw out your best thinking and fully address your idea. Ones that provide an answer to your ideal client's problem or highlight a solution that you are specifically able to talk about.

These questions will highlight YOU doing your best work (you in concert pitch).

But you're not done...

From here, you need to do an 80/20 analysis of your questions (and the answers to the questions) and NICHE, down to the very specific TOPICS you are going to share in your book.

Usually a theme will jump out at you, but the rule of thumb is it needs to follow these 4 criteria for your book to be the most compelling to your ideal client:

1) Be simple to understand

2) Have a significant benefit

3) Be interesting

4) Have some element of surprise, unexpectedness, curiosity; an aha moment

**Next, you will determine the format you want to use for your book.**

This is how you structure your topics so they follow a logical path.

Important: You want to structure your outline based on what you can discuss during a 2 hour interview. Don't try to cram too much into your book; it will backfire on you. If you really want to share more, make it a series of books.

The very best way to do this is to make sure your book is hyper-focused around ONE main message. This means that you *focus on getting your ideal client to believe or understand just ONE thing*. That's it!

Of course, all your content needs to be a stand-alone valuable product with a valuable message (regardless of whether your prospect decides to do business with you). You don't want any gotchas or "sales messages" in disguise here...

For example, maybe you want to educate someone on your unique process, system or product. Or you may want to show people how to solve a specific problem, or you want to highlight a solution you can provide.

The best way to get clear on this concept is

to design your book so that you give your prospects exactly what they WANT—the answer(s) to their burning questions, FOR FREE (just like I am doing with the 5-Hour Author).

Yes, I know the thought of giving all your best stuff away for free (in a book) is a bit scary, but it's the only reason to author a client-getting book. Sure, there are exceptions, albeit few and far between.

So, unless you have some special chicken recipe, like KFC, go ahead and share it already.

**Here's a simple (and very effective) format that you can use to lay out your book:**

1) Introduce the Big-Ass Problem or the Big-Ass Opportunity (your ideal clients have).

2) Agitate the Problem or shine a light on the Opportunity (what happens when they don't fix the problem they have or what happens

when they take advantage of this opportunity).

3) Offer the Bigger Solution (this happens to be what you provide—no selling here, please).

4) The Conclusion and your Offer to Help (why you are the clear choice to solve their problem—this can be on the back cover as well).

5) Your "About" Pages[1] (this is where you will woo your ideal clients by highlighting how you can help THEM; you'll also point out some credibility-boosting stuff about you, your business and your team).

6) Acknowledgements.

These topics will become the chapter or section titles of your book's table of contents AND the source of the questions you will answer (to generate your book's content) in Step 2.

---

1. www.YourAboutPages.com

## The Offer to Help

Now that you have your outline and format, you can easily zero in on what you can OFFER your ideal clients that is good for them (and good for you!).

You'll want to start by making sure what you are sharing in the book elegantly leads up to your offer at the end of the book (because the reader must be compelled to want to take the next step).

A great way to do this is to visualize what would be the NATURAL next step for them to take, the step that is good for them (and is super-easy to take).

For example: You can offer to help them with X, and they can find out more about X by email or phone, or by finding information on a website, completing a form, etc.

## The Title Of Your Book

Once you know what your book is going to

be about, you'll need to spend some time coming up with the very best title. The title is made up of two parts, what I refer to as THE HEADLINE and SUBHEADLINE.

The title and cover of your book matter. A LOT.

In fact, I believe your cover is the most important part of this entire process because even if your book is very good, which it will be, your cover (alone) can determine 80% of the success of your book.

Why is this? Because we all judge a book by its cover. And the truth is most people will get a book because they want the benefit that is advertised on the cover. That's it!

**The first rule of thumb here is this: Your headline needs to stand on its own.**

... The best way to do that is to make sure your headline, in and of itself, is going to cause your ideal clients to say, "I gotta have it! I gotta have it!" The headline must scream to the reader "That's for ME," and it's got to tell the WHOLE story (without the story having to be read).

Once the headline is read, there shouldn't be anything else needed to get the person to understand the benefit your book is offering.

So how do you come up with the perfect attention-grabbing headline for your book (the headline)?

Well, there are many ways, but here's my favorite formula for generating the perfect headline and TESTING ones that you have already thought of (I learned this from Gary Bencivenga).

## The formula is Benefit + Curiosity = Interest (B + C = I).

Let's break this down...

**Benefit:** This is your main benefit that speaks to the desired end result (what your ideal client wants or needs, your proof or promise to them. It should be direct and descriptive.

+ *(Plus)*

Curiosity: It has to be unpredictable. "Predictability kills curiosity."

= *(Equals)*

**Interest:** You must have the benefit AND the curiosity or you'll lose interest.

**A very relevant example is the 5-Hour Author headline. It explains the main benefit, it's descriptive and it ignites curiosity.**

Getting the headline just right is easier said than done, but when you do it, your ideal clients will want to drop everything and get your book immediately.

But there's one more step!

Once you've come up with a headline that passes the TEST and has your ideal client

INTERESTED in your book, the next step is to create a subheadline.

When used effectively, a headline and subheadline together are an unstoppable combination. But it's critical to create a headline that stands on its own first, before adding a subheadline. The reason for this is that the only function of subheadlines is to add meaning, interest and/or value to the HEADLINE. So you should use it whenever you can make the headline better. That's it.

Here are the best ways to use a subheadline to make your headline better:

- Use it to further define and add clarity to your headline.
- Use it to segment your target audience and call out to your ideal clients directly.
- Use it to highlight, heighten and enhance the interest that's already been created from your headline.
- Use it to narrow or broaden the

focus of the benefit offered in your headline.
- Use it to appeal to your ideal clients' senses by helping them imagine what it would be like to get the benefit you are offering.
- Use it to add more value to the benefit offered in your headline. This is like putting your ideal client's interest on overdrive or fast-forward, or adding a bonus.

Let's use this book as an example: The 5-Hour Author: How to Author a Client-Getting Book in Just 5 Hours… The headline passes the TEST and stands on its own, but the subheadline makes the headline better. The first way it makes it better is by further defining the book's target audience: It calls out to business owners who also want to get more clients, not to people who want to author fiction, a biography or a memoir. The next way it adds more value is by setting expectations for the target audience. It accomplishes this in 3 ways. The first is by adding "How to." Because I know the majority of biz owners don't know how to author a book, this lets them know that this book will teach them how. The second is by reiterating that it takes "Just 5 Hours." This adds to the curiosity and helps minimize concerns about the huge time commitments that come with writing a book. The final benefit of this subheadline is its ability to help business owners envision what it would be like to get more clients when they become an author.

A book with a masterfully crafted headline and subheadline is The 4-Hour Workweek: Escape 9-5, Live Anywhere, and Join the New Rich by Tim Ferriss.

If you're getting stuck with finding the right words to use in your subheadline, here's a fallback method: Try using "How to".

- Or The 5 Ways to X (insert your benefit)
- Or The 5 Reasons to X
- Or Why X

This method works well because these phrases use magical gateway words that scream "educational content." When your ideal client is looking for what you offer, education is the key to showing off what you know and why you're different. Education is the great neutralizer that can elegantly lead your ideal clients to your services and products.

Here's a great example (used frequently in marketing circles) of just how much of a difference the title of your book MAKES. It's from published author Naura Hayden.

The first edition of her book, published in 1982, "*Astro-Logical Love*" was "Unique" but was lacking the "I gotta have it" effect—selling just under 5,000 copies.

The book was republished in 1998 (same book, just a different title), "*How You Satisfy a Woman Every Time...and Have Her Beg for More*!" was a home run—selling over 2.5 million copies!

Of course, the above example shows book sales (a very tangible metric). But imagine how many more clients the right title and cover would get you…

So here's a quick exercise you can do to see if your book's title passes the test. Get at least 20 people to give you feedback on your title. You can talk to them, send it by email or post the headline on a social network. But just say, "Hey, I am finishing a book," and let them know the title (headline and subheadline) of the book only (no explanations). And then ask the question, "Are you interested?" That's it. If the first thing they say is, "What's it about?" then you probably don't have the right title. Yes, for some people that may be a natural response (without really thinking first), so be alert for any false alarms. But in general this will be a good test for you.

**When it comes to your book cover design, less is more.**

The best way to frame this up is to use this example: Your book cover should be like a well-done billboard that you drive by on the highway—you have only a few seconds to see it, read it and understand it. Unfortunately, most billboards still get this wrong, and so do authors.

A perfect cover has few colors, and has big, clear and readable fonts that will catch your readers' attention. And it uses images sparingly (I prefer ONE meaningful image).

Your book cover will usually be tiny when showcased on your website and used in advertising, or if you submit it to any of the online bookstores. So big lettering and a bold image are important. And because you want to make sure the title of your book is prominently displayed and readable, even when your book is the size of a thumbnail image, it's not always possible to fit a headline and subheadline on the cover together. In these cases, I recommend only displaying the headline on the cover, and making sure to draw attention to the subheadline on your website, advertising and online bookstore.

When you pull off the perfect title and cover design, your clients will be lining up to get your help.

**Take a break from doing anything on your book. Let the thoughts, topics and ideas simmer a bit.**

Next, we're going to jump back in with a clear mind and look at the draft you created so far. Now you can spend the next hour digging deeper and polishing your purpose, the topics, the outline, the headline and the offer you are going to make at the end of the book. Then you'll spend the final hour going through the process with a fine tooth comb, one last time.

When you're done you'll emerge with a final outline, headline and offer that you're bursting with enthusiasm to share.

I do recommend that you add two more sections to your book. The first is for your "about" pages, where you can tell the reader about your business and you. The "about" pages aren't for spewing out the typical business jargon like name, rank and serial number. They should be value-laden and focused on how your business serves your ideal clients most selfish desires. Then you'll spend a few minutes sprinkling in some cool stuff about you and tooting your own horn in the "about the author" part.

The other section is for the "acknowledgments". This section is where you can thank people, organizations and companies that have helped you out in some unique way that's worth sharing.

One last thing, double check all your topic areas to make sure they tie into the big benefit that the title/headline of your book is promising.

Okay, now you should have a final outline, topic areas to discuss, and a headline and your offer (what you're selling). Time to move on to Step 2.

## Focus Tips //

I don't know about you, but there are times when I struggle with getting (and staying) focused, particularly when I am working on projects that require lots of deep and creative thought. My favorite way to get into the zone is to listen to music on the Focus@Will app or their website.

I simply select the type of music I want to listen to and how long I want to focus. The service does the rest. It really helps me get into deep levels of concentration, which makes me more productive in less time.

Focus@will is a neuroscience-based music service that helps you focus and reduce distractions. The technology is proven to extend your attention span and productivity cycles.

Try it out at www.focusatwill.com.

Another focus hack that works for me is using the Momentum extension for Google

Chrome. Whenever I open a new tab in Chrome, I see an inspiring reminder of what I want to do that day. Not a gateway into the internet black hole. This simple tweak reminds me to stay on track. It prevents me from being sucked into the constant loop of checking email. And keeps me from jumping online for something that's usually not important.

Try it out at momentumdash.com.

9

# STEP 2: CREATE YOUR BOOK

---

Get your unique knowledge out of your brain and into a book.

Time Invested — 2 Hours

Action Steps:

1) Find your voice.

2) Record your book's content (**write like you speak**).

3) Submit your interview to be transcribed. (send to www.rev.com)

In this step you will get your book's content out of your brain and into a book. You will do this by having someone interview you (using the questions you created in Step 1) and recording the audio of your session. This can be your assistant, a business partner, or a peer, preferably this should be someone who's got some biz know-how and can keep your interview flowing and on track.

This step is simple. You're going to answer the questions (from your outline) that you already prepared and draw out your expertise, through your VOICE.

The very best way to communicate your message (your unique perspective) is through your voice.

By recording yourself, you will be writing your book just like you speak.

Although the title of this section sounds a bit daunting, the process is quite simple. That is IF you have done the work in the last section to get super clear on your topics and outline.

If you still have some doubt, then it's important that you spend a few more minutes polishing the topics you'll be talking about in this section. If you spend a little more time in Step 1, no worries, you may have a chance to make up time later in this process.

You gotta make sure your outline is perfect (not bloated) and that it's focused around ONE main message that you can talk "intelligently" about. This means that you focus on getting your ideal client to believe or understand just ONE thing. That's it!

BUT before we get into creating your content, let's spend a few minutes finding your voice (your unique perspective).

## Find Your Voice

Once you know WHAT you're going to talk about, HOW do you get your unique knowledge out of your brain and into a book?

This is where we ALL get tripped up, so here's a tip to get you started (and make sure you're sharing your best stuff)...

I recommend that you take a few minutes to think through HOW you are going to talk about your idea and lock in your perspective.

Your ideal clients pay you for only ONE thing, and that's your perspective.

Yep, they want to know your unique perspective MORE than anything else...

But why is your perspective so important? It's my belief that there are really NO new ideas. Every idea is just a combination of other ideas.

So don't get hung up because someone else already thought of your idea, or on wondering if your idea is the best... you need to focus only on WHY your perspective is the best.

Once we turn the corner with this way of thinking, the message becomes clear and more clients will come knocking.

## Let's get started creating your content (write the way you speak)

It really is this simple: you're going to be answering the questions you've already prepared that are related to the outline you've just created.

Your interviewer will help you draw out your book's content by asking you about the topics/questions you prepared in Step 1. They will also keep you on track by managing the interview steps. This way you don't have to stress about what's next on the outline or dwell on any of the minutiae. All you have to do is show up and TALK. The right interviewer will elegantly guide you through your interview—resulting in a book draft that can easily be molded into a masterpiece.

As mentioned in Step 1, the suggested interview length is 2 hours. If you prefer, break it up into 1-hour sessions. Remember, your interview should only be as long as it takes to cover the topics you have thoroughly outlined. I just found the sweet spot to be around 2 hours of interview time.

When doing this interview, imagine yourself sitting one-on-one with your ideal client; or if you prefer, imagine you're with a close friend—do whichever makes you feel more comfortable. Don't imagine that you're speaking to a large crowd; this is just an intimate conversation.

No excuses—you've already prepared the topics, and now you just have to be yourself and share all your best stuff. All you have to do is TALK. If you mess up or—more appropriately—when you mess up, stumble, or say

"UM," don't sweat it; this will all get transformed in Step 3 when you get this into the hands of a professional writer.

When you get into a groove, you'll be surprised (and proud) of what comes out of your subconscious mind. I like to relate this to being a top improv actor. Think about it—they don't prepare at all, they can't. They just show up and it's amazing to see what stories they create and weave together. In this case you're already well prepared and you're the best at what you do. You just have to get your story out.

The key to jumping on the same creative super-highway that the top improv actors use is to say YES to your own voice. Often the logical lies we put in place hold us back from our more creative selves. When you know your stuff and you get into the flow, it's truly amazing what goodies will come out through your voice.

Of course, you are going to record the interview. There are several tools you can use and several different ways you can get interviewed. One way is to use Rev Voice Recorder. It's available on the Web at www.Rev.com and on iTunes and Google play.

**Here's a tip to help map out your interview:**

Make a bulleted list below each of your interview questions/topics with any reminders and/or subtopics that you want to discuss (any stuff that you don't want to forget). Make sure they're in sequential order. Think of these bullets as tiny breadcrumbs that help you stay on track during your interview.

One of the ways I make sure my outline is perfect is that I play a virtual tennis match with my ideal client (these days I prefer a Pickleball match). I think of the questions that my client is asking me about the problem they want to solve or an opportunity that I feel it's my duty to share with them. The tennis match is simply a way for me to visualize the back-and-forth "volley" that I am trying to achieve. It helps me get clear on what I will say (and do) and then how my ideal client would respond back to me. That response would lead to the next question on my outline. I use this way of thinking until I have succeeded in helping my ideal client believe or understand the ONE thing that either they need a solution to OR an opportunity that they shouldn't miss out on.

Another great way to tackle the interview process is to split your topics and subtopics into separate bite-size interviews. This is really easy to do because you can "pause" the recording anytime, then pick up where you left off. The point is that you can get as granular as you wish. And regardless of which tool that you use, any delays in the recording will be removed once the interview is transcribed into text.

**Humanize your message:** It's a little weird that I have to bring this up, but some people (me included) have a tendency to go into expert mode during this type of interview. Now that's not necessarily a bad thing; it just means you get so focused on delivering value that you can temporarily forget to be the chummy human being that you are. But when you throttle back the prescriptive mind-set and humanize your message, you bring your book to life and ultimately create a deeper bond with your readers, who are already hardwired to tune in to personal accounts...

This is a great example of something that you should embed into your outline, where you want to interject a story, cite an example, share a case study, or highlight a personal account or a testimonial of some sort. Something is valuable to share if it's timely, relevant and moves your book forward. Don't overthink this; keep your personalizations to the point and follow this simple formula to easily become more interesting. It's from the Nobel prize-winning poet Rudyard Kipling: "I keep six faithful serving men who teach me well and true. Their names are What and Where and When and How and Why and Who."

Marketers and journalists refer to this as the "5W1H" formula for investigating any topic. It's quite useful in telling stories, creating outlines and the like.

Here are some of my suggested tools to record your interview on the computer or over the phone:

- Uber Conference
  www.uberconference.com
- GoToMeeting by Citrix
  www.gotomeeting.com
- OpenVoice by Citrix
  www.openvoice.com
- Skype Call Recorder for Mac
  www.ecamm.com/mac/callrecorder
- FaceTime Call Recorder for Mac
  www.ecamm.com/mac/callrecorderft
- Google Hangouts
  www.google.com/hangouts
- Free Conference Call
  www.freeconferencecall.com

- GarageBand
  www.apple.com/mac/garageband

Of course, there are several phone systems that have the ability to record your phone calls. I prefer to use systems built on Twilio www.twilio.com. The one that I recommend is Fix Your Funnel www.fixyourfunnel.com.

**Dictation:** Dictation will not work for this type of creative exercise. Unfortunately, dictation software and apps won't allow you to speak freely and capture everything that you say with 99.9% accuracy. Sure, dictation is great and has its purpose. But to make it work you have to change how you speak to cater to the dictation software. You'll find yourself starting and stopping often; that alone will kick you out of any creative flow that you're trying to achieve. When you record the audio, you can speak freely, fast or slow, start and stop whenever you want to, and capture everything you say.

Now it's time to take the first step to convert the spoken word to the written word and get your interview transcribed into text. If you used Rev.com for the audio recording, then all you need to do is submit the recording to be transcribed, directly from the app or on their website.

I use the Rev app to record other content as well—very handy...

## More About REV //

Rev is the trusted source for all your audio (and video) transcriptions and language translations. I recommend their service because it's easy (and superconvenient) to use from their mobile app (and to record your voice while on the go) or from any computer. And with the click of a button you can have the Rev team transcribe your voice into text—usually within a few hours...

Plus, they translate over 30 different languages, so you can rely on their network of tested and rated professional translators with your books, special reports, white papers, resource guides, instruction manuals, brochures, courses, blog posts, articles, speeches and presentations.

The quality of their work is excellent, and they'll complete your request fast and at a good price. And another big reason to use them is their service is secure, so you can trust them with your important business information. Find out more at www.rev.com

# STEP 3: POLISH YOUR BOOK

> "The only kind of writing is rewriting." – Ernest Hemingway

## THE PROCESS OF CONVERTING YOUR SPOKEN WORDS TO WRITTEN WORDS, AND FINDING THE PERFECT WRITER FOR YOU...

# The rewriting process, and polishing your work of art.

**Action steps:**

1) Lightly polish your book's draft (edit, tweak, add or remove anything from your book).

2) Personalize your book's content.

- Add the intros and outros to elegantly marry all your chapters together.
- Add the chapter title, chapter headline and subheadlines.

3) Search and identify a professional writer at WriterAccess.com.

- Recruit and short list two-to-three writers.
- Test your writer candidates by having them rewrite a small piece of your book's draft.

- Hire your writer and submit your book draft to be rewritten.

4) Submit your final book draft to the editing team at WriterAccess.com. I also recommend ProofreadNOW.com for professional editing and proofreading.

The interview is complete…and, you have the recording transcribed into text.

At this point, you may still be saying to yourself, "How is a recorded transcript going to turn into a great book?" Well, the truth is, you already have a BIG head start when you get your books outline (and the questions your book is going to answer) polished up in Step 1. When you do your work in Step 1 everything will just flow nicely (trust me). But, you're right, your rough draft will definitely need an extreme-makeover after you've recorded your interview in Step 2. That's why it's called a rough draft. The key to transforming the spoken word into the written word is a professional writer. Remember: Great writing is rewriting.

At this point your book draft is just like a supermodel getting ready for the runway. Your book's content is stellar, but it still needs some necessary polishing to be runway ready. Just as a supermodel needs the makeup artist, dress rehearsal and choreographer before the show, your book needs deeper scrubbing, structuring, rewriting and some final touches before it hits the bookshelf.

BUT before you reach out to a writer there are some loose ends to tie up. By doing a few small tweaks upfront, your process of engaging a writer will be even smoother.

The first thing that you're going to do is proofread your draft for accuracy and any inconsistencies. You'll find the low hanging fruit and make any high-level corrections along the way.

## Personalize your book draft.

The next thing you will do is personalize the

draft by adding the intros, outros, headlines, subheadlines and chapter titles. These personalizations are the first step to improving the flow of your recorded transcript and giving it a more book-like structure. The goal of this step is to add personal touches that will draw the reader into the content and elegantly marry each chapter together. These personal touches will also break your rough draft into neatly organized chapters, topics and subtopics. Obviously, the personalizations you make now will be subject to change, editing or deleted as you move through the book-creation process. But doing this now will help you get belly to belly with your writer. More personalizations will be needed once you have a final draft of your book. Cool? cool.

**Let's start with the intro's and outro's.**

The intro's and outro's are the ways to introduce (intro) a topic and to marry your interview sections together (outro). Once you read your draft, you'll know exactly what I mean. There needs to be an elegant way to join all your topics together into an excellent story to allow the book to flow. Most of the time your intros and outros will only need to be a sentence or two. An example would be a sentence that says, "In the next section I'll discuss X" or "... you'll learn X." And in some cases it could even be a short phrase. An example would be, "Coming up...", "Next", or "Onward." There are two exceptions to these examples; one is the "introduction", how you start your book and the other is the "conclusion", how you end it. These two areas will require a little more detail to elegantly tie everything together.

You'll add the intros and outros to your book draft and then move to the next step...

**Next up... Chapter Titles, Headlines, Subheadlines and Formatting.**

Chapter titles, chapter headlines, subheadlines and purposeful formatting (highlight...etc.) should convey the key storyline and benefits in a flowing manner.

Let's start with your chapter titles.

I recommend you make your chapter titles short and punchy. They should be easy to understand and should convey the benefits of that chapter—something that creates the desire in your ideal client to read the chapter. I prefer shorter chapter titles because they get to the point and, frankly, they make your table of contents and chapter titles streamlined in your finished book.

Next, fill in your chapter headlines and subheadlines.

The way to draw the reader in and further expand on the short chapter titles is to use a chapter headline. The headline will be your way of setting up the chapter and framing the content for your ideal client.

Your headline goes hand-in-hand with subheadlines.

The subheadlines are integral to a well-done book. They are the glue that holds the chapter together and what sucks your readers into your chapter and then keeps them interested. When the subheads are done correctly, they will tell the story of that chapter even if all the other text were removed. When perfected, someone could just skim over your chapter to decide if they're interested. Think of your subheads as a greased slide your ideal client will come down naturally.

**Formatting with a purpose.**

My advice with formatting is simple, "Don't go overboard". For example, most times highlighting or bolding single words is a recipe for overstimulating your reader. Although the use of formatting is a personal preference, my opinion is that formatting should be used sparingly. There's just one exception and that's bullets. When used properly, bullets will draw your reader in and deliver your key points on a silver platter. Bullets act like magnets that attract even the laziest, uninterested readers – but only if they are relevant and packed with goodies that help your reader. If not, using bullets will hurt you. The best filter to determine how you use formatting is to make sure it's purposeful. My recommendation is that you should limit your use of formatting to bullets, italics or capital letters for emphasizing single words, and bold or underline for complete phrases. As you've probably noticed, I use all CAPS (quite a bit) to emphasize single words. Everyone has their own style, just find what works for you.

Here's the deal—when done properly, your headlines, subheadlines and formatting will prepare the readers, draw them into your chapter, add emphasis, and draw attention to the key points (of the page), benefits or the offer to help your ideal client.

When you get it right, the result will be a chapter that is easier on the eyes and visually appealing; you will increase the focus on your message and enhance the overall improved flow and reader experience.

**NOTE:** The 5-Hour Author process will produce a REAL paperback book that's the perfect size for paperback and digital books. Of course, there are several factors that will determine how long your finished book is: the length of your interview, how fast you speak, any additional sections that you add to your book, how much writing and editing is done to your rough draft and how you format your book.

## The Art of Revision

OKAY, now it's time to get your draft into the hands of a professional writer. You've already done 80% of the work, and now it's time to hire the big guns to clean it up, polish and marry everything together for you. I recommend WriterAccess.com to locate a professional writer.

**Here's why:** WriterAccess has attracted some of the best US-based writers. You can locate the professional writers you need by their skill level, performance and customer reviews. I recommend using their 6-star writers for your book, which will ensure that you get top-shelf writing. This includes but is not limited to writing brand-new content and weaving it into your draft, reworking your draft to make sure it delivers a clear and cohesive message, and rewriting and editing your content for improved flow and impact.

Because you'll be delivering a tight-knit book draft that has a laser-targeted message and is 100% YOU, a professional writer will quickly be able to follow your book's TONE and STYLE, which will make it much, much easier for him or her to transform your audio conversation to the written word. In fact, once you zero in on the perfect writer, you'll get a book that's so authentic your own family, friends and business associates won't believe you didn't write it.

Getting started with WriterAccess.

You can start by signing up for a free account just to test drive their platform, but when you're ready to start your book I strongly suggest that you sign up for their Plus Service. To put it simply, the Plus Service is for people who are serious about time, money and authoring a client-getting book. With the Plus Service, you will get a dedicated Account Manager who will do a kickoff call with you to learn about your requirements and your goals, and who will then work closely with you to find the perfect writer for your book. The great part about the Plus Service is that it doesn't cost you anything extra. It's based on the amount of money you plan to spend with WriterAccess, and in the case of the Plus Service, it's a deposit of $2,500. Coincidentally, the cost to rewrite, edit and proofread your book will be in the same ballpark, so why not take advantage of their concierge-like service? And if you don't use all of this money or any of it, no sweat, just get a refund or apply any extra funds to your future projects. WriterAccess guarantees your happiness anyway, so you're doubly protected...

*Here's what I recommend you do at WriterAccess...*

**Recruiting the perfect writer for your book.**

Just as in any other industry, the most talented writers are not seeking out work, they're being sought out. So the best way to find a writer will be through direct recruitment. Besides the fact that WriterAccess has the largest pool of top writers, they also have a slick platform that makes it easy to source and recruit the best talent for your needs. Their platform gives you the power to search and connect with only the writers that match your requirements (or if you use the Plus Service, to search with the assistance of your dedicated Account Manager).

WriterAccess also has a unique feature called Casting Call. This is a sophisticated recruiting tool that allows you to share the details of your book project with specific writers at WriterAccess who can apply for the chance to work with you. Email notifications are sent out to the writers who have the proficiency and industry expertise required (as indicated on their profiles), and they can respond with details as to why they're the best fit. I recommend using a Casting Call if you have not had success finding a writer directly.

**Put them to the test.**

Once you've narrowed the writer pool down to two to three prospects, the next step is to find out who's the best fit by putting them to the TEST.

The way to do this is to simply give the writers a small assignment that will test their writing skills and help you find out who's the most qualified for your book. I suggest having them rewrite the same 300-500 words of content, something from the beginning of your book (based on your directions, specifications, project details, etc.). Give them a day or two to complete the assignment, then pick the winner. This is a low-cost method to ensure that you have a writer who will produce the best results for you. Plus, this test will kick-start the rewriting of your draft.

Be up front with your writer candidates. Let them know that you're indeed trying them out and this is just a test to see if it's the right fit for both of you. Simply let them know that they're competing with a couple other writers and if they're the right fit for the job, then they will receive the remainder of the assignment. If for some reason this test does not uncover an acceptable candidate, it could mean you need to revisit your project details or simply rinse and repeat another test. But if you spend the time up front narrowing down your candidate pool and clearly defining your project, you won't have any problems.

**Hire your writer.**

Congratulations, you found a writer. The next thing you're going to do is hire that writer through the WriterAccess platform to complete the rest of your book.

The rule of thumb is your 5-Hour Author-style book should take approximately 2 weeks for your writer to complete. Of course, you'll ultimately determine this by communicating directly with your writer and your Account Manager (if applicable). In the end, it's all about good communication and setting appropriate and achievable expectations for all parties. For example, be clear that you expect your writer to continue this assignment within 3 days of the hire date. Let your writer know that he or she has 14 days to deliver your final draft and then 2-3 days to make any revisions that you request.

Once you've delivered your rough draft and clearly outlined your goals, requirements and time line, you'll work closely with the writer on the iterations of your book draft.

When you get your final draft back, you will review it and make any necessary tweaks before you send it off for editing.

**It's time for professional editing and proofreading.**

Once all the revisions are complete, the next thing you will do is send your final draft off to a professional writer for editing and proofreading. No good book can exist without good editing, so don't shortcut this step, EVER. Why? The only thing that makes good writing better writing is better editing. The editing will also improve the flow of your book, and it will enhance the overall message of your book. Think of editing and proofreading like getting a second opinion.

First off, it's easy to jump back in and place an editing order with WriterAccess. They have a dedicated team of editors that go through your book with a fine-tooth comb checking for spelling, grammar, clarity, tone and style.

Or another service I recommend is the professional writers at ProofreadNOW.com. With ProofreadNOW's Level 1 service, two professional editors will read and review your book for clarity, as well as suggest changes and corrections.

The great thing about both of these services is that you'll see the BEFORE and AFTER version of your draft as part of their service. The editors will provide you with suggested changes and comments that you can review and compare, then you can quickly make the changes and revisions needed to ensure you have a literary masterpiece.

**Tips on how to work with your writers.**

Although your draft will tell a lot about your tone, style and overall storyline, it's best to communicate as much as possible so you can be 100% sure to locate the best writer and editors for your book.

That means the more you give them, the more you'll get. Start this by typing up a project description that clearly outlines your job, requirements, specifications and any comments you want them to read before they start working from your draft or editing the written book. For example, let them know that the assignment is to rewrite your book's draft that was created from an audio interview, or, in the case of the editor, to proofread the rewrite. Tell them your intended audience, your ideal client avatar. Tell them the industry you're in. You can give them an idea of the tone and style you desire for the book, things to add, things to avoid and more. And don't forget to let them know when you need it. Name the deadline and the best workflow, including how much time you need for review, revision and approval. When you send them your draft, let them know ALL your requests so they can make every attempt to conform to your wishes. Just as with any successful project you embark on, the foundation is good communication. So be willing to build a good relationship and a rapport, and take an active role up front with your writer and editor.

You're almost to the finish line! Now it's time to finalize and publish your book.

Onward...

## More on Writer Access //

Why do the best companies rely on WriterAccess? In minutes, you can access over 10,000 US-based writers, then pinpoint the exact skills and industry experience you need. Plus they have a fantastic support team and an easy to use web-based platform. And they guarantee that you'll be delighted with the results you get or you don't pay! Get started at www.WriterAccess.com

## More on Proofread NOW //

ProofreadNOW will proofread your business documents 24 hours a day, 365 days a year. An important feature of their service is that every document you submit is reviewed by two expert editors, and then sent back to you via a secure server—within a matter of hours or days (your pick). This double review is a standard part of their service, and there is no additional charge for this. What this means is you can trust them to catch the mistakes that you could otherwise miss on your own.

They have two levels of service that you can choose from:

- Level 1-Clarity checks for spelling errors, punctuation errors, typographical errors, and grammar errors. (Recommended for The 5-Hour Author).
- Level 2-Style includes their Level 1 service as well as content editing and rewriting.

Find out more at www.ProofreadNOW.com

## Automated Editing Tools //

**Grammarly:**

Grammarly is an automated proofreader that follows me around all day. It makes me a better writer by finding and correcting my mistakes. It even gives me occasional word suggestions so I can sound more intelligent...

Grammarly is like a Big Brother for your everyday writing and communications. It even follows you around the internet. So whether you're writing an email in Gmail, sending someone a message on LinkedIn or writing a letter, Grammarly's got your back. But aside from their intelligent software robot that helps fix and diversify your writing. They also have professional proofreaders available to double-check your most challenging assignments. Check it out at www.Grammarly.com

**Hemingway App:**

Hemingway scans and analyzes your writing then highlights the areas that need improvement. It points out wordy sentences, adverbs, and passive voice. It also identifies the unnecessary words and phrases that are getting in your way. Allowing you to write with power and clarity.

A powerful combination. I love to use Grammarly's grammar and proofreading features inside Hemingway's online editor. Get started at www.HemingwayApp.com

**Audio On Demand:**

One of my favorite ways to review my work is to use the SPEECH function on Mac computers. I highlight the text that I want to listen to, select the "Speech" option and then "Start Speaking". I can listen to it right away, or I can select "Add to iTunes as a Spoken Track" if I want to save it as an audio file. I can quickly identify any inconsistencies that I didn't catch during the reading process. Plus, when I listen to my content it puts me in the shoes of the reader...

There are also mobile apps that do text-to-speech. The one I use is Voicepaper. I like it because it reads my notes and documents directly from Evernote and Dropbox. You can check it out at VoicepaperApp.com.

# STEP 4: PUBLISH YOUR BOOK

The final steps, cover design and publishing your shiny new book...

**ACTION STEPS:**

1) Format and publish your book as an ebook

and a paperback book using PressBooks.com (making the inside of the book look good).

2) Copy and paste your final book draft into PressBooks.

3) Design your book's cover—start a 7-day design contest at 99designs.com (making the outside of the book look good).

Now you're going to review the final content one more time, make any minor changes that you need to make and then begin formatting it. I use and recommend PressBooks to publish an entire book. You'll be able to export the book in multiple formats for ebooks and printed books. There are no technical skills required to use this service. In one word, it's... AMAZING. To get up to speed on setting up your book visit PressBooks.com/Help

Now it's time to get the outside of your book looking like a million bucks! The best way to do this is to launch a design contest on 99designs, where dozens of top designers will compete to create your ebook and printed book covers. In fact, the 5-Hour Author artwork was all done through 99designs.

The key to making sure your design contest is a huge success is to explain clearly what you want AND what you don't want on your cover. Remember, the designers are not marketing experts, they are design experts.

The first thing you will do when you start a design contest on 99designs is write a design brief. This is a list of questions that you'll answer with as much detail as possible. An effective design brief gives designers everything they need to know to exceed your expectations. Of course, you'll want to refer to my cover design recommendations in Chapter 8, Step 1 for help completing your design brief.

It's important to know that you'll need two separate versions of your cover design: one for your ebook and one for your paperback (printed book). Yes, the professional designers will already know how to do this for you...

But you will need to provide them with a little information to get started. You will need to let them know the cover size and your book's total number of pages so that they can calculate the total dimensions of your cover and the spine for your paperback book. For this reason, it's important that you publish your book in PressBooks prior to launching a design contest at 99designs. This way you will know the size and the length of your book. For example, I recommend using the cover size of 5 inches by 8 inches (5"x8") in PressBooks. I also recommend a cover design with the title of your book and your name displayed on the spine (Amazon's CreateSpace requires your book to be at least 101 pages to have any writing on the spine).

Once you have your book nicely formatted and you've selected your cover design, there's a special feeling you'll have that you simply can't ignore. I can tell you from experience that you'll be bursting with excitement and enthusiasm (I remember the feeling while I write this... aaah). It's the kind of feeling that makes you want to run outside and just scream as loud as you can... YEAH!!! Or, in proper terms, this is the point in the authoring process when you realize it was freakin' worth it.

## More About PressBooks //

PressBooks is a simple book publishing platform for ebooks and print books. Think of it as your online book manager where your finished book can be created and managed from one simple web-based platform—no technical skills required. PressBooks is the future of book publishing because it empowers individual authors to control the book publishing process while avoiding the high cost and time-consuming nature of book production.

Simply put, PressBooks creates the files you need to publish your books and ebooks: PDF for print and print-on-demand, including Amazon's CreateSpace; ebooks including MOBI for Kindle book publishing; and

EPUB for Apple's iBooks, Nook, Kobo and others.

PressBooks solves the typical production problems that come with the publishing of books. And it's built on top of the world's largest (and most trusted) web platform—WordPress. With over 50 themes available, you'll be sure to find the perfect one that makes the inside of your book look great.

PressBooks does not create book covers—you'll need to source those separately—but it does include your ebook cover in ebook file exports. PressBooks also includes an easy way for your ideal clients to read your book online and/or where they can buy your book. The easy web interface will also allow you to make unlimited changes and exports of the print-ready and digital formats of your book.

Get started at www.PressBooks.com

## More about 99designs //

99designs is your one stop shop for anything graphic design related. Their community of nearly 1 million designers will create dozens of designs for you. Then you pick the winner. Plus they guarantee you'll find a design that you love or your money back.

Get started at 99designs.com

## Alternate Cover Design Options //

I realize there are lots of other cover design options available to you. I have worked with many designers over the years. I have also used several Photoshop-like design tools. In the end, the crowdsourced book covers at 99designs.com is an excellent choice. But I'll share a few more options that I give a thumbs up.

Another company I recommend for designing your book cover is OctagonLab.com. The neat thing about OctagonLab is they only do book covers. And more important, they know we all judge a book by its cover. So they will design a book cover based on what will attract your ideal clients.

My favorite do it yourself nontechnical design tools are MyeCoverMaker.com and Canva.com. If you do plan to go the DIY route with your book's cover design, the webpage to calculate the size of your paperback book cover and download your cover design template is Createspace.com/Help/Book/Artwork.do.

12

# STEP 5: LAUNCH YOUR BOOK

## The launch of your new book.

**Action Steps:**

1) Export your completed book in three formats from PressBooks.com to cover all your publishing and distribution needs.

2) Set up the single-purpose landing pages for your book using LeadPages.com. I also recommend ClickFunnels.com.

3) Integrate the book into your biz marketing campaigns and conversation channels.

4) Build a client-getting machine around your book that attracts your ideal clients, builds rapport, converts sales and generates referrals.

5) Submit your book to major book retailers (optional).

Now that you have a completed book in all possible formats (Kindle, iBooks, Nook, etc.) and a great book cover, the next step is to export your finished book from Press-Books so you can begin getting the word out.

PressBooks will generate the three different file formats (with a click of a button) that will cover all your publishing and distribution needs.

## Here's how you'll use the three different book formats:

PDF — Of course, this version is the most versatile, since it can be read on any device or computer. But it's also the print-ready version of your book. You'll use this file to publish your paperback book on Amazon.com using their CreateSpace.com service. Once you publish your paperback book on CreateSpace, it will be available through Amazon and their many distribution channels. As the author, you're also able to order copies of your paperback book from CreateSpace at a discount.

Because the PDF version is easy to share via a download link or email, it's great to use on a single-purpose webpage as a free or paid download.

EPUB — This version is used by all the major ebook distributors (except for Amazon's Kindle). For example, this version can be read on Apple devices and computers as well as most devices and computers with an ePub app or software download. It can also be read on Barnes & Noble's Nook and Kobo. The best way to use this format is through Smashwords.com. Their service will distribute your ebook to over a dozen online retailers.

MOBI — This is Amazon's proprietary ebook format and can be read on the Amazon Kindle app or any Amazon Kindle device. You'll use this format to submit your ebook to Amazon's Kindle Direct Publishing.

**Important:** When you export your ebook from Pressbooks, the EPUB and MOBI versions will already include the image of your book cover. This will not be the case for the print-ready version of your book—the PDF file. For this version, you'll need to upload two separate files to CreateSpace. One will be the PDF file from PressBooks (the inside pages of your book), and the other will be the PDF file from 99designs (the cover of your book).

How do you plan to use your book to get clients?

Based on the goals that you have for your new book, you can choose to submit your book to the major book sites, or you can simply integrate it into your day-to-day business as a lead generator, educational tool, etc. It's perfectly normal (and not uncommon) to decide not to sell or distribute the book through mass distribution sites. This is up to you. The digital versions of your book will work on all devices and apps regardless of whether you submit them to the major ebook distributors.

But even if you choose not to distribute your book on a broad scale, you'll still want some paperback copies on hand. In this case, you can have your book printed by a print-on-demand company. One that I use and recommend for this is 48hourbooks.com.

Regardless of which path you decide to go down, you will need paperback books, from either CreateSpace or a company like 48-Hour Books, that you can hand out and send out to your ideal clients. As covered earlier, you'll also want to give away the paperback book (for free or for a small fee) on your single-purpose webpage in exchange for your target prospects' contact information. Or you can just charge for the shipping costs of the book. The reason you can't afford to skip this step is that when you successfully marry the process of giving away your high-value book with an expertly crafted direct marketing campaign, you'll find yourself talking to all the right-fit prospects.

Once you implement and optimize this campaign, you may find it cumbersome to manage the fulfillment side of things, particularly if you don't have the systems in place to take care of the shipping and handling. Or maybe you just don't want to fuss with it.

In this case, I recommend using an all-in-one

fulfillment partner like Corporate Disk Company Disk.com. They will make your life much, much easier because they can MAKE and DELIVER your book for you. Yes, they can print your paperback book in-house, or you can send them bulk copies of your book from CreateSpace. Either way, they'll send it out on your behalf and even send any other goodies that you want to ride along with it. And most likely their systems can talk to yours, so any orders that come can instantly be sent to Disk.com (I know their systems sync up with the Infusionsoft software I use to run my business).

Because there are many benefits to submitting your book to the major book sites, it's likely that you'll utilize their broad reach as one way to get the word out about your book.

**When you decide to use the major book sites, get an ISBN and ASIN.**

An ISBN (International Standard Book Number) is a unique identifier associated with your book. ISBNs can be a lot of trouble and very confusing to most authors, so here's the best path for you to follow…

You'll want to get an ISBN for your EPUB and PDF formats of your book. The quickest, easiest, cheapest and most-recommended method is to get an ISBN directly from Smashwords and Amazon's CreateSpace at the time you complete your book submission. When you're done you'll have an ISBN (a 13-digit ISBN) associated with your EPUB format from Smashwords and two ISBN's (a 10-digit ISBN and 13-digit ISBN) attached to your PDF format at Amazon's CreateSpace.

An ISBN is critical (in my opinion) because some of the major retailers such as Apple and Kobo will not accept your book on their platforms without one. Although there are several benefits to an ISBN, this is the #1 reason to attach an ISBN to your book.

An ISBN is not needed for your MOBI format that is used when publishing through

Kindle Direct Publishing. In this case what you will receive is a 10-digit ASIN (Amazon Standard Identification Number), which is unique to your eBook and found on Amazon's Kindle platform.

It's also important to note that publishing your book with an ISBN from a reputable company like Smashwords and Amazon's CreateSpace doesn't have anything to do with the ownership or copyright of your work. You still have complete control over all your content; you're just not listed as the publisher. The same goes for publishing your book with an ASIN on Amazon's Kindle platform.

Again, here are the major platforms that you should use:

- **CreateSpace by Amazon** — submit your paperback book. Use the PDF format of your book. Visit www.CreateSpace.com
- **Kindle Direct Publishing by Amazon** — submit your Kindle

ebook. Use the MOBI format of your book. Visit https://kdp.amazon.com
- **Smashwords** — use to distribute your ebook to all major book stores (except Amazon Kindle). Use the EPUB format of your book. Visit www.Smashwords.com

## AT FIRST, IT'S ALL ABOUT THE MARKETING.

There's only one thing that makes a great book work for you, and that's marketing.

Obviously, the marketing phase is an ongoing process. What I have outlined here are some of my favorite marketing tactics to get the word out about your book. Marketing tactics are commonplace. What determines their success is knowing how to implement, test, trigger, and modify these tactics. Over the years, I've learned several marketing lessons the hard way. Most of my mistakes could be avoided by doing three things.

1. Advertise to the right people. Who sees your message determines at least half of your advertising success.
2. Ad copy that talks directly to your ideal client most selfish desires. Your ad must have the right message, be results-driven and include psychological triggers. This formula will make it irresistible for your ideal clients to get a copy of your book.
3. Ask for your ideal clients to take an action.

Your direct marketing efforts usually start with setting up a single purpose landing page where people can get a copy of your book (either for free or how they can buy it).

I use and recommend LeadPages.net and ClickFunnels.com. I recommend having two versions.

The first will be a simple book landing page (also known as your client-getting magnet).

Like the one at 5HourAuthor.com/Simple. The second will be one that is more authoritative. The purpose of this page is to share more detailed information that positions you as the celebrity, the authority and the specialist of your niche. Like the one at 5HourAuthor.com/Authority.

Here are a few ways to flex your marketing muscles and get the word out about your book (for long-term effectiveness these tactics should be part of a well-defined plan):

Share Your Book: Share it with your networks (business associates, networking groups, joint venture partners, trade shows, social media assets, viral giveaways, and blogs).

Notify Your Mailing List: Notify your current list by email, direct mail, phone, text message then use the same follow-up process you use for new leads. To manage my conversation channels, I use the all-in-one customer relationship management, sales and marketing and e-commerce software from

Infusionsoft.com. I use it in conjunction with GoogleApps to run most of my business. The other all-in-one system I recommend is Ontraport.com.

**Online Advertising:** An effective online advertising campaign starts with running text and display ads on the major networks. There are dozens but over 90% of the traffic is on Facebook.com/advertising, Google.com/advertising, and Bing.com/advertising.

Another option is to buy advertising space on niche and mass-media websites. Either through direct media buying or a syndicated platform. Besides 99designs.com, an excellent site to get your advertising banner ads done for you is 20DollarBanners.com.

**Offline Advertising:** Print media still outperforms digital media for several services and products. My favorite thing to do is marry offline campaigns with online media. Embed your book in trade magazines, newsletters, newspapers, etc.

**Direct Mail:** I love direct mail. If you're not already a fan of direct mail, it's because you haven't perfected it yet. Sure, it's clunky and old school but it doesn't have to be. Once you have the right list and then the right messages you'll be addicted to the results direct mail brings. An effective way to get the word out about your book is to design a series of greeting cards, postcards, and letters. Mail them to your clients, prospects and targeted lists, etc.

I use ZenDirect.com, SendOutCards.com and Click2Mail.com to send cards, postcards, letters and even the occasional gift. What makes these services even better for me are the software integrations from ZenDirect, SendOutCards (software integration by FixYourFunnel.com) and Click2Mail that tie my direct mail campaigns into Infusionsoft and GoogleApps. Allowing me to 100% automate the sending of snail mail for my business.

Integrate your new book into the marketing

of your business, at all touch points. For example, try using your book as a sales escalator. By selling a low-priced item (like your book) that has a much higher perceived value, you'll establish trust AND you'll consummate a business relationship with your ideal client. The great part about this small transaction is that it will serve as an escalator for this client to make more frequent and higher-priced purchases from you. When you use your book as a sales escalator, I recommend using a fulfillment partner like Disk.com to package and deliver the book for you.

Get honest feedback on your new book. Send your new book to at least 5 of your ideal (and most critical) clients, either ones who have paid you to help them already or ones who have shown an interest in working with you. You want to ask them for specific feedback (good and bad) on your book.

Also, I recommend identifying partners, vendors and other raving fans who will themselves benefit by helping you get more exposure for the book.

Once you've used Marketing Muscles[1] to attract your ideal prospects and start, continue or re-start conversations. You'll need to master your Conversation Channels[2] because most of your ideal clients will not be immediately ready to buy from you. So you need a system to continue nurturing the potential buyers in your network. This "touch strategy" allows prospective buyers to be kept abreast of current and relevant information so that they remain engaged up through the time they decide to buy. That's why it's crucial to build a Client-Getting Machine[3] around your book that attracts your ideal clients, builds rapport, converts sales, and generates referrals.

I look forward to hearing of your success. And don't forget to share your new book with me. You can send me an email to

1. www.MarketingMuscles.com
2. www.ConversationChannels.com
3. www.ClientGettingMachine.com

Travis+Author@TravisJohn.com, I'll respond personally.

Thanks!

## P.S. Here's how I can help you right now.

You already plan to be an author—you even have ideas swirling around in your head of what your book can be about. But how do you make sure you have an idea worth doing[4]? That's where I come in.

My mission is to help already successful business owners, entrepreneurs and independent professionals author their first client-getting book. As part of my commitment to us reaching this goal, I'd like to help you come up with the perfect idea for your book. This way you can reach more clients and make a greater difference, in less time.

…Successful people don't struggle coming up with ideas. They struggle finding ones worth

---

4. www.IdeaWorthDoing.com

implementing, which is why most books never get started. I've already given you the implementation PLAN. I've shared with you WHO can help you with your book. Now all you need is an IDEA worth doing.

And because I have a knack for uncovering the best ideas, I've set aside time to talk with you so I can help you draw out your very best one.

I'll work with you to identify the unique things about you and your product, service or business. Stuff you've done, accomplished, pioneered, overcome, etc. It's likely we'll reveal some things that you completely forgot about, even things you didn't realize were remarkable.

The ONLY goal of this collaborative process is to help you come up with an idea worth doing. I know that once you discover the perfect idea, there will be no stopping you…

…If you'd like to make sure you have an idea

worth doing or need some help coming up with a new idea, then I'd like to help!

To get started, please send me an email to Travis+Idea@TravisJohn.com, and we'll take it from there...

...There's only one thing better than a good idea: a better one.

## P.P.S. If you like what you've read, then go VIP.

Join us in the VIP room to get exclusive offers and updates to the 5-Hour Author, plus other forward-thinking ideas and fresh biz perspectives from me personally.

It's 100% free. When you join us, you'll lock in your spot and be guaranteed to get my best stuff. Stuff that you can use in your biz right away.

If you'd like to join, then send me an email to Travis+VIP@TravisJohn.com and I'll take it from there...

## P.P.P.S. SHARE THE 5-HOUR AUTHOR WITH SOMEONE LIKE YOURSELF.

If you know one person that would benefit from a client-getting book, you can email them a complimentary copy of the 5-Hour Author. The email has already been prepared for you, just add their email address and hit SEND. Visit www.5HourAuthor.com/Gift to give away a copy of the book.

*Wait!* Check out the bonus chapters to get the scoop on turning your new book into an audiobook. Or find out how you can create a book by using the content you already created. Or how to author your book in multiple languages. Or how to create other business assets using the 5-Hour Author blueprint. Tune in to the next section to learn all about it.

# PART II

# BONUS SECTION

# CREATE AN AUDIOBOOK

## Create an Audio Version of Your Book

Congratulations. Your book is complete, but there is one more thing that I highly recommend you do—create an audio version of your book.

Before I get into the process, let me first say that the creation of an audiobook can be a completely different animal. However, I have simplified this process for you, 5-Hour Author style. The one and only goal here is to give you the easiest and most effective way to create a quality audio version of your book. Once you're done, you'll have all the media covered with your new book—you'll have multiple digital book formats, a paperback book and an audio version. Creating multiple media options will make it even easier to distribute your book, which will ultimately allow you to reach more of your ideal clients.

Don't ignore audio. Although more people prefer to read books, there's a large segment of people who will actually listen to your book, and if they like it, they'll also get a copy to read or vice versa. Then there are the audio enthusiasts who simply prefer to consume information in audio format. There are plenty of people in this category who want what you are SELLING, but they will never hear your message unless it's on audio. So let's get started.

Here's what to do.

Step 1: Make sure you are 100% done with your book. This sounds obvious, but you don't want to record your audiobook over and over, starting from scratch every time you make a change. Or have to send your recordings off to an editor every time you make a change. So the best practice is to make sure you are done squashing any bugs, and you have made all your minor tweaks, etc.

Step 2: Just record yourself reading your book, one chapter at a time. Practice reading each chapter out loud and lock in the nuances of the timing and punctuation before recording. This is important because how you read in your head and reading out loud have entirely different punctuation and timing. So the best way to pull this off without major modifications is to read your own book instead of hiring a narrator. You know your content inside and out, so reading your own book out loud will come naturally for you.

I recommend that you use your computer to record the audio. You don't need to get fancy, BUT I strongly suggest using a high-quality, studio-style microphone and finding a small, quiet room or even a closet so you can get the best acoustics without all the fuss. Another tip is to do your recording at night when there are fewer noises. The audio will be an hour or two long, and of course you'll use it with your digital and paperback book—as an educational tool, lead generator, add-on or bonus, etc. For example, you can embed it on your website or share a download link when someone gets a digital or paperback copy of your book.

When you record your own audiobook, you'll create a deeper connection with your ideal clients because they will appreciate the authenticity, enthusiasm and emphasis that only you (and your voice) can bring to your book. Also, when you read it yourself, you'll find it natural to improvise in the cases where the printed word and spoken word are not in sync. So don't get hung up on whether you have a radio voice. Just read the book and be yourself.

Tools I use.

I am an Apple user, so the tools I use to record audio are GarageBand and QuickTime. Another tool I use is Audacity; it works on Mac and PC. Then I export or convert the file to MP3 format.

When it comes to microphones, there's no shortage of opinions on what microphone is the best. But everyone tends to agree, there's NO one size fits all. There are many factors to consider when selecting a mic to record your audiobook. These factors include:

- Price
- Quality
- Convenience
- Size
- Where you plan to record audio

- How much background noise you'll be competing with
- Your other recording tools
- Your voice type

But the mic is not the only part of making great audio. The other half of your sound quality is about HOW you use the mic—AKA working the mic. For that reason, I prefer inexpensive but good-quality portable microphones. The one I use is Audio-Technica's ATR2100 USB Dynamic Mic. It's an excellent microphone that doesn't need an elaborate setup. Plus it reduces any unwanted sounds caused by room noise and background noise.

Some people believe you will get a better recording experience from condenser mics. But they are sensitive to external sounds and need a more controlled recording environment. Compared to dynamic mics, I found you'll need to spend more money on the mic and have an elaborate setup to notice any difference in sound quality.

If you would like to distribute your audiobook on iTunes, Audible and Amazon, a little post-production will be needed to polish the audiobook before you put it out there. I recommend finding someone who's familiar with the editing functions of Audacity, GarageBand or QuickTime and who can prepare the audio files to meet the required specifications for those platforms. The good news is that once you have completed the light editing of your audio files, there's a one-stop service to publish your audiobook on all these retail sites.

**Introducing Amazon's ACX.**

If you would like to get massive exposure for your audiobook through Audible.com, iTunes and Amazon.com, then your best option is to use Amazon's ACX platform www.acx.com. Without question, the ACX platform is the easiest and most comprehensive way to self-publish audiobooks. With ACX, you'll get a professionally produced audiobook, one that has multiple chapter breaks and one that is formatted for iTunes, Audible.com and Amazon.com. Plus, it's simple to do. Just claim your book title on ACX, upload your recordings and start promoting your audiobook. That's it.

I realize that recording an audiobook can still be a daunting task. So if you do prefer to have someone else narrate your audiobook (professional voice talent), then ACX makes this a piece of cake too. You can find professional narrators, hold auditions and make a deal to get your audiobook produced directly on ACX.

# AUTHORITY TO AUTHOR

## THE 3 WAYS TO AUTHOR A BOOK USING YOUR AUTHORITY OR SOMEONE ELSE'S.

There are 3 different ways to use *authority* to become an author. (I have already shared with you the *first* way (extensively) and that's to use your own authority to become an author.)

If you still haven't started on your book, or you want to know of "optional" shortcuts, here they are.

1) **You are the Authority** — you draw out your book's content from your own knowledge and expertise, through your voice (BEST).

2) **You are NOT the Authority** — you can co-author a book with an expert/authority on the topic that you want to cover.

Why would you do this? This is an excellent way to open up a new line of business, develop a new niche, go deeper into a service you already provide, etc. By co-authoring the book with another authority that has complementary skills to yours, you establish the same credibility and rapport that you would if you were the only authority.

You may already have someone in mind. If not, the best way to connect with the authority you need is through high-level networking groups.

If you choose to pursue this option, you can follow the exact steps outlined in the 5-Hour Author.

3) **Assets to Author** — use the stuff you've already created. You already have written articles, documents, blog posts, essays, and white papers; done presentations; and made audios and videos, etc.

Why not use the content that you've already GOT to make your book? And do what I call *Assets to Author*. Using this option is like doing an extreme makeover of your existing content. *The most common application of this method is a Blog to Book...*

You'll simply follow the same process you used in the 5-Hour Author, except in Step 2 you'll be using existing content instead of drawing out the content from your own voice.

**Here's the summary** of what to do if you decide to use the content you already have on hand:

1) Gather the assets that are on the topic you want your book to be ABOUT.

2) Lightly edit, tweak and remove anything you don't want in your book.

3) Add an intro and outro, headline, sub-headline and chapter title to each section (this is to elegantly marry everything together).

4) Optional: Send your rough draft to a professional writer at WriterAccess.com.

5) Send your final book draft to the editors at WriterAccess.com or ProofreadNOW.com for additional editing and proofreading.

6) Publish your book using PressBooks.com.

7) Get your book's cover designed using 99designs.com.

8) Get the word out about your new book.

Here's to publishing your client-getting book super-fast!

ered from having your book translated
# GLOBALIZATION

Another critical task is preparing your book for international markets and taking advantage of the big wide world of opportunities. The world is flat when it comes to connectivity and international business, and now it's easier than ever to get your book translated into another language—and go global.

Once you have determined that you would benefit from having your book translated into another language (or multiple languages), I suggest you submit your completed book to Rev's translation team. They translate over 30 different languages, so you can rely on their network of tested and rated professional translators to make sure the message of your book remains intact.

Get started at www.rev.com

# THE ART OF WRITING

The process of writing, particularly writing a book, is artful, beautiful, powerful and sacred. The 5-Hour Author is just a different way to utilize the beauty of the written word, not to knock the skill of being a good writer. In fact, I think mastering the written word is one of the most challenging but most rewarding and timeless skills, and I think everyone should consider doing it. Unfortunately, I know it's simply not in the cards for everybody. That's why the 5-hour Author can be the next best thing for you, maybe even a gateway for you to get addicted to writing. For those who already like to write, this can serve as a guide to being more creative and productive.

The best way to share a message long and far IS, and has always been, with a BOOK. This started with the Bible. I firmly believe that most problems in your life and business can be solved by being a better communicator, and the written word is where it ALL starts. Do I think that I am a good communicator, a good writer? Not yet, but I'm always working on my craft.

## There's Hope For Everyone.

I always hated to read, much less write. I was a terrible student all the way through school and college—so bad that I was thoroughly embarrassed about my past self until I realized that the school system and process were more screwed up than I was. So, after I got the much-needed entrepreneurial therapy along with the right mentors, I was able to get on the right path to being a lifelong student. But this time it was on my terms.

Go forth and create something, my friend. Something that is full of YOU...

# IT'S NOT JUST FOR BOOKS

I want to share something cool with you.

... Maybe you've already figured this out, but the 5-Hour Author is NOT just for creating books.

It's also a whole new way of thinking about how you create your STUFF.

You can use it to create special reports, white papers, resource guides, instruction manuals, courses, demos, workshops, case studies, blog posts, articles, speeches and presentations...

What are you going to create first?

# CROSS PROMOTION

## Cross Promotion

When it's appropriate, you should highlight other services and products that you offer or recommend. Using this cross-selling strategy can be an effective way to:

- Educate your ideal clients about your other areas of expertise.

- Provide suggestions on related services or products.
- Give more depth of what you do.
- Endorse a service or product that you recommend.

# Return On Author (ROA)

## What's Your Return on Author?

This book has exposed the logical lies that hold most people back from being an author. It's simplified the authoring process. It's provided a step-by-step plan to create a client-getting book without all the fuss. Plus it's revealed the many benefits of being an author...

...BUT what's the REAL return on being an author? Well, here's a quick look at potential financial returns.

Example 1:
Let's assume your book could get you 5 ideal

clients per year. Ones who are worth $5,000 to your business (their lifetime value). Of course, that's equal to $25,000—not bad.

Now let's take into account that a client-getting book has a 10-year shelf life. If you could generate the same amount of business for 10 years, that would be a quarter of a million dollars. All of this from just ONE book.

Now let's step it up a notch...

**Example 2:**
Instead of 5 ideal clients, what if you were able to get 10 new clients per year? Ones who are worth $10,000 to your business. That's a cool $100,000. But if you could generate the same amount of business during your book's 10-year shelf life. That would be a whopping one million dollars!

Now it's your turn. Take a few minutes to plug in your numbers and forecast your "return on author" (ROA).

# 5-Step Checklist

## You're already successful at what you do.

Successful people are successful because they always seek out the highest-quality advisors. For this reason, I think every author needs an agent. Nothing weird; in the self-publishing world, your agent is simply someone who will support you through the authoring process.

In the case of the 5-Hour Author, I have provided you with a step-by-step guide for your agent to walk you swiftly through the process. Your agent will be another set of eyes and ears to keep you accountable, a proofreader and someone with whom to bounce around your ideas. The right agent will help you draw out your best stuff, keep you on track and ultimately ensure your success.

You may already have someone on your team, a top assistant, a business partner or a business associate. Of course, it would be a plus if you had someone who's biz-savvy, has some marketing know-how or understands the book-creation process.

With any project, it's easy to get off track (or even give up), but when you have someone guiding you and keeping you accountable, it's much easier to succeed and a lot harder to say "I quit." Plus, by attaching a name and label to the role, whomever you select as your agent will want to rise to the occasion and pour everything he's got into seeing your finished book. Let's go.

# The 5 steps to author a client-getting book can be categorized by these 6 P's:

1) *Productize* your knowledge in the form of a book
2) *Produce* your book
3) *Personalize* and *Polish* your book
4) *Publish* your book
5) *Promote* your book

**Step 1: Productize your knowledge, in the form of a book**

- The purpose of your book.
- The very best idea for your book (what's your book going to be about?).
- The questions your book will answer (what's the ONE thing you want your ideal client to believe or understand?).
- The ideal client avatar (with WHOM (exactly) you want to have a conversation in your book).

- The outline, topics and format that will provide an optimum reader experience.
- Niche down (polish and organize your topics into the best possible format).
- The interview questions that you will answer in Step 2.
- Draw out the most compelling offer for your book (how you or your product can help your ideal client).
- The perfect title for your book.

Step 2: Produce your book

- Find your voice.
- Record your book's content (write like you speak).
- Submit your interview to be transcribed. (send to Rev)

Step 3: Personalize and Polish your book

- Lightly polish your book's draft (edit, tweak, add or remove anything from your book).

- Personalize your book's content.
- Add the intros and outros to elegantly marry all your chapters together.
- Add the chapter title, chapter headline and subheadlines.
- Search and identify a professional writer at WriterAccess.
  - Recruit and short list two-to-three writers.
  - Test your writer candidates by having them rewrite a small piece of your book's draft.
  - Hire your writer and submit your book draft to be rewritten.
- Submit your final book draft to the editing team at WriterAccess or ProofreadNOW for professional editing and proofreading.

Step 4: Publish your book

- Format and publish your book as an

ebook and a paperback book using PressBooks (making the inside of the book look good).
- Copy and paste your final book draft into PressBooks.
- Design your book's cover—start a 7-day design contest at 99designs (making the outside of the book look good).

Step 5: Promote your book

- Export your completed book from Pressbooks.
- Set up single-purpose landing pages for your book using LeadPages or ClickFunnels.
- Integrate the book into your biz marketing campaigns and conversation channels.
- Build a client-getting machine around your book that attracts your ideal clients, builds rapport, converts sales and generates referrals.

- Submit your book to major book retailers (optional).

*Get the word out about your new book:*

- Share it with your networks (business associates, networking groups, joint venture partners, trade shows, social media assets, viral giveaways, and blogs).
- Identify partners, vendors and other raving fans who will themselves benefit by helping you get more exposure for the book.
- Notify your own mailing list by email, direct mail, phone and text message about your book.
- Use Facebook, Google and Bing's advertising platforms to place targeted ads for your book.
- Send out targeted greeting cards, postcard and letters for your ideal clients to get a copy of your book.
- Embed your book in trade

magazines, newsletters, newspapers, etc.
- Get feedback on your book from at least 5 of your ideal clients.

**Additional:**

- Create an audio version of your book.
- Articles to author—repurpose the content you already created.
- Create other "client getting" resources using the 5-Hour Author.

Here's to superfast publishing of your first client-getting book!

# Tools and Resources

## Recording Your Interview:

- Rev
  www.rev.com
- Google Hangouts
  www.google.com/hangouts
- GoToMeeting by Citrix
  www.gotomeeting.com
- OpenVoice by Citrix
  www.openvoice.com
- Free Conference Call
  www.freeconferencecall.com
- Uber Conference
  www.uberconference.com
- Skype Call Recorder for Mac
  www.ecamm.com/mac/callrecorder

- FaceTime Call Recorder for Mac
  www.ecamm.com/mac/callrecorderft
- GarageBand for Mac
  www.apple.com/mac/garageband
- Fix Your Funnel
  www.fixyourfunnel.com
- Twilio
  www.twilio.com

## Transcription and Translation:

- Rev
  www.rev.com

## Writing and Editing:

- WriterAccess
  www.writeraccess.com
- ProofreadNOW
  www.proofreadnow.com
- Grammarly
  www.grammarly.com

- Hemingway App
  www.hemingwayapp.com

## Design:

- 99designs
  www.99designs.com
- OctagonLab
  www.octagonlab.com
- $20 Banners
  www.20dollarbanners.com
- Canva
  www.canva.com
- MyEcoverMaker.com
  www.myecovermaker.com

## Book Publishing and Fulfillment:

- Pressbooks
  www.pressbooks.com
- CreateSpace
  www.createspace.com
- **Amazon Kindle Direct Publishing**
  https://kdp.amazon.com

- Smashwords
  www.smashwords.com
- 48-Hour Books
  www.48hourbooks.com
- Corporate Disk Company
  www.disk.com
- CreateSpace (calculate the size of your cover and spine)
  https://www.createspace.com/Products/Book/CoverPDF.jsp
  https://www.createspace.com/Help/Book/Artwork.do

## Getting The Word Out:

- LeadPages
  www.leadpages.net
- ClickFunnels
  www.clickfunnels.com
- Infusionsoft.com
  www.infusionsoft.com
- Ontraport
  www.ontraport.com
- Facebook Ads
  www.facebook.com/advertising

- *Google Ads*
  www.google.com/advertising
- *Bing Ads*
  www.bing.com/advertising
- *Click2Mail*
  www.click2mail.com
- *Send Out Cards*
  www.sendoutcards.com/travisjohn (send a free card, it's on me)
- *ZenDirect Cards*
  www.zendirect.com
- *Fix Your Funnel*
  www.fixyourfunnel.com
- *NextMark*
  http://lists.nextmark.com
- *PR Web*
  www.prweb.com
- *iReach by PR Newswire*
  https://ireach.prnewswire.com
- *WebWire*
  www.webwire.com
- *Sniply*
  www.snip.ly

## Audiobook:

- Rev
  www.rev.com
- GarageBand for Mac
  www.apple.com/mac/garageband
- QuickTime for Mac
  www.apple.com/quicktime/extending
- Apple iTunes
  www.apple.com/itunes
- Amazon ACX
  www.acx.com
- Audible
  www.audible.com
- Audacity
  www.audacityteam.org

## Productivity:

- Focus@Will
  www.focusatwill.com
- Voicepaper
  www.voicepaperapp.com

- MomentumDash
  www.momentumdash.com

# Acknowledgements

As with all my endeavors, the first and most important acknowledgment goes to my wife and kids, who are the center of my universe and the source of all my passions. And who always forgive me for the times I am out—working on my craft.

Then there are all my fellow entrepreneurs, extended family members and friends who gave me a strong support system as I worked on this book.

A special shout-out to the entrepreneurs and thought leaders whom I gain inspiration and valuable insights: Joe Polish, Dean Jackson, Dan Sullivan, Peter Diamandis, Frank Kern, Brendon Burchard, John Carlton and Tim Ferriss. Thanks to you all.

Then there are the visionaries and technologists, Jason Chicola of Rev, Byron White of WriterAccess, Hugh McGuire of PressBooks and Matt Mickiewicz and Mark Harbottleof 99designs that created the tools and services I wrote about in this book. Without them, this innovative approach to publishing a book would not be possible. Thank you for your willingness to put it — all on the line — and invest in the "future of publishing". Because of you more people can author a book without all the fuss. Also a big thumbs-up to Rob Barnes for working with me to create a bulletproof plan to success at WriterAccess.

A huge extra thanks to my wife, Tonya, and to the editors at ProofreadNOW.com, who forced me to focus and relentlessly polish this book.

Finally, I want to acknowledge you, reader, for giving me your time and allowing me to share this new solution with you. I hope to hear from you soon.

# About the Author

## Travis's story

A father, husband, perpetual traveler, minimalist, runner, health geek, adventure seeker, RV enthusiast, unschooling parent, pioneer, street-smart entrepreneur, writer and author of the future, Travis has designed a life that allows him to stay sane, be present with his family and work with clients he loves.

Travis is the founder and chief strategist of Travis John Agency LLC. He is an innovator and well-known marketing and sales strategist who spends most of his time helping Already Successful™ small business owners, entrepreneurs and independent professionals with strategic decisions, marketing direction and the innovation needed to ensure ongoing success.

Simply put, Travis has a knack for finding unique ways to increase sales and solve top-shelf business problems. One way he helps clients achieve lofty goals is by building them client-getting machines. Machines that attract ideal clients and close more high-value sales in less time, with less effort.

Travis believes the single best gift people can give the world is to bank on themselves. He found by investing in the skills that add value to his clients he was investing in their success. Thus, creating a greater return for everyone. One of the ways Travis banks on himself is by running a results based business. One that rewards him only when his clients get results.

Travis's entrepreneurial DNA became apparent in early childhood while he was doing everything from selling baseball cards and his parents' crap at the flea market to cutting his friends' hair in his garage and running a neighborhood lawn business. From there he has never looked back. Although he went off-course a few times, what remained constant was his ability to develop new ideas and see ways to put them to good use.

Other successful small-time ventures followed, but this pattern was one he would finally harness later in life. He is a late bloomer and an underdog, but he's got long-distance stamina (he won the mini marathon in 5th grade and later received a college scholarship for track and cross-country). Whatever Travis put his mind to, whether it was selling baseball cards or customizing his first car (Nissan Pulsar NX), he showed great potential at a young age. Without realizing it, he was creating the blueprint for his later successes.

After graduating from the University of North Florida with a bachelor's degree in health science, he cofounded Virtual Health, a preventive health services company that provided workplace solutions. He went on to work for one of the largest technology services companies in the world. As a sales manager there, he specialized in delivering IT solutions to Fortune 500 companies, generating tens of millions in revenue at a time for some of these businesses. Working long hours, he made his employers rich, while his own health and spirit began to deteriorate.

Fast-forward five years—he was still working nonstop, this time in the distressed property market. As the founder of one of the first real estate short-sale agencies, Travis was quoted in publications such as *The Washington Post*, and he devoted most of his time to finding solutions for homeowners who had financial issues. Travis was fully immersed in the distressed property world, and he eliminated over $50 million in negative equity in Florida alone. At the same time, he founded a national referral network; a title and escrow agency; an advanced real estate sign installation business; and a real estate transaction service for attorneys, homeowners and real estate brokers to process paperwork and make routine bank calls. He then founded Short Sale My Yacht and became one of the first people in the country to apply real estate short-sale techniques to luxury items.

Although most people would have considered Travis successful (especially in the midst of the worst housing market ever) something was missing. Then it dawned on him—he had stumbled on the very thing that brought his success. It was MARKETING and his obsession with figuring out what actually drives business success. There was a direct correlation to his success and his passion to learn and implement the marketing and sales strategies that triggered exponential growth in his biz.

But Travis still struggled to connect the dots.

In January 2010, when the world was still on the verge of an economic collapse, Travis and his wife, Tonya, had their third child. This event created a radical shift in Travis's mindset and he got clear on what life meant to him. Through this soul-searching, he realized his one-of-a-kind business experience and marketing know-how were extremely valuable—stuff that the RIGHT people would benefit from immensely. So that's exactly what Travis did. He narrowed the focus of his business to working ONLY with people he can be a hero to. Ultimately, he discovered his unique ability lies in his capacity to develop tools, programs, products and services that add value to Already Successful people and their businesses.

Another big catalyst that pushed Travis to hyper-focus was his introduction to *The 4-Hour Workweek* by Tim Ferriss. This book opened his eyes to what he was good at and what made him happy.

But more important, these life-altering events were a wake-up call for Travis. He has always created life on his terms, but here was a reminder that he had fallen a little off-course. It was the kick in the pants that Travis needed to fine-tune his business around both his unique strengths and his lifestyle goals.

Travis has found that clients are attracted to working with him because of his natural ability to see opportunities before others do and then understand what it takes to nurture and develop these ideas—using his entrepreneurial instincts and marketing prowess to apply them.

Since falling in love with marketing, Travis has invested thousands and thousands of hours (and dollars) on mastering his craft, seeking out the best masterminds and mentors in the world. As a student of marketing, Travis is doing his best work when he's using his marketing muscles—whether it's identifying a new idea that doubles a business's revenue in 12 months or honing an entrepreneurial idea of his own that gives life to a new product or service.

Made in the USA
Charleston, SC
05 September 2015